MARCIA WALLACE

don't look back,

we're not going that way

MARCIA WALLACE

don't look back,

we're not going that way

(... or how I overcame a rocky childhood,
a nervous breakdown, breast cancer,
widowhood, fat, fire and
menopausal motherhood
and still manage to count
my lucky chickens.)

Don't Look Back,
We're Not Going That Way

PUBLISHED BY
Off The Wall Publications
5482 Wilshire Blvd., #1557
Los Angeles, CA 90036
INTERNET: www.marciawallace.com
E-MAIL: MW@MarciaWallace.com

COVER DESIGN
Russ Hardin

COVER PHOTO
Allison Reynolds

BOOK DESIGN AND PRODUCTION
Alan Bernhard, Argent Books, Boulder, Colorado

Printed in the United States of America

ISBN 0-9748305-0-X
Library of Congress Control Number: 2003099509

W*ith appreciation*

and love

to my sister Sherry.

contents

Appreciations ix

1 Toto, We're Not in Iowa Anymore 3

2 A Rocky Road, and I Don't Mean Ice Cream 13

3 Fast Times at the Dairy Queen 29

4 Sunny Los Angeles 41

5 Bad Sex in the City 63

6 Bad Sex in the City, Part 2: Looking for Mr. Close 71

7 I Got Rhythm 83

8 I Got My Man 91

9 A Funny Thing Happened on the Way to the Altar 101

10 Our Love Is Here to Stay 111

11 Meant For Each Other 117

12 Mad About the Boy 131

13 It Can't Happen to Us... 139

14 ...But It Did 147

15 Dying Husbands, Real Estate and the L.A. Riots 157

16 In Pieces 165

17 Our House 173

18 Unforgettable 181

19 On the Road Again 185

20 Coming Together 193

21 Sing It, Frank! 199

22 Starting Over 207

23 Christmas 1998 215

24 Christmas 2000 219

Epilogue 223

appreciations

Two years ago I said to no one in particular, "This is my first book; please be kind," and boy did the universe respond with the gifts of time and talent from friends who are also wonderful writers, editors and artists. I offer such gratitude to:

Russ Hardin for the cover design. The man can do anything.

Rosemary Rogers, whose proposal got the ball rolling (I didn't have a clue how to write one), part of which you can read on the back cover and also on my website.

Valerie Watson, who is still standing after her final edit. My tense impairment alone would have broken a lesser person.

Dean Williamson, wherever you are, who thought I had a story to tell. Ditto Carmen La Via and Cathryn Michon.

Alan Bernhard, for the patience and education.

Betsy Hailey, for her endless encouragement.

Howard Borris, for more than there's room to list.

Brett Somers, for thirty years of best friendship.

And finally . . . such love and gratitude to John and Natalie Bates. This book would never have been written without your vision, talent and support.

This book would never have been published without the same from W. Bruce Cameron.

Thank you, thank you, thank you.

O kay, here's the deal.

I never sat down one day and said, "I think I'll write a book." I think of myself as an improviser, a storyteller, a speaker. In my speaking travels around the country, members of the audience would say, "Don't you have a book? If you had a book, I'd buy it."

So I sat down to tell the story of my life. It includes some letters. It starts with my decade in New York and then it goes back to my childhood and starts from the beginning. The good news is it sounds just like me, and the bad news is it sounds just like me … sometimes all over the place.

I think I touch on some interesting experiences and observations. It's a bit of a stream-of-consciousness thing, and like all streams, sometimes the waters are clear, and sometimes they're a little murky. (I love a lively metaphor, don't you?) Anyway, here we go.

⟶

1 don't look back

→

Toto, We're Not in Iowa Anymore

Christmas 1964

Dearest Wendy,

Well, I'm here. Two weeks ago we were student teaching in Keokuk, Iowa, and now I'm in the Big Apple. I took off for New York City the day we graduated from college. I weigh two hundred and thirty pounds and have a hundred and fifty dollars in the bank. Oh, all right, I suppose my ready cash should at least equal my weight, but what the hell, I've always had more guts than brains.

My first week here I bought a three-dollar seat behind a pole to see Funny Girl *and was thrilled beyond belief. Next I saw* Hello Dolly *and thought, "Well, I can play that chubbette role." So I called the David Merrick office and asked for an audition. Who knew you weren't supposed to do that? They said, "Um ... okay." Only one pesky problem; I kind of forgot that I can't really sing. But I prepared a rousing rendition of the ever-lovely "Oh, My Feet," and I took off to the St. James Theater with my accompanist Bobby Gorman. I was definitely not good, but I was loud—so loud I couldn't hear the woman when she kept yelling, "Thank you, that'll be all. Thank you!" In fact, I think I was still singing (euphemistically speaking) as she left the theater muttering, "Thank you, thank you, that's enough, thank you ..."*

Not an ideal entrance into the musical theater, but was I

3

discouraged? Au contraire. To quote that old philosopher, Poke Wallace: "Don't look back, we're not going that way."

On second thought, that happened my second week in New York. My first week, I got arrested. I was staying with the only people I knew in the city, my friends Dick Natkowski and Carlton Davis, and went around the corner for a little snack. Well, this supermarket was as big as my hometown and I was beside myself; so many snacks, so little time. Anyway, I ended up with an armful and put a big package of M&Ms in my pocket, forgot they were there, paid my bill and walked out on Broadway.

The minute I left the place, two guys clamped their grubby mitts on my shoulders and said, "Come with us." They took me to the basement of Key Food, where the one guy said, "I seen you when you came in and you looked shifty." They made me sign a paper saying I would never darken the door of their store again. "Sign it," they said, "or we'll call the police." They also took my M&Ms. "Well," I thought, "that's it. I can't be a star now. I have a record, and when I'm famous, I'll end up on the cover of some trashy tabloid."

Well, since now I was practically a felon and clearly wasn't going to be a musical comedy star by Tuesday, I had to get me some jobs. I've had several; I substitute-teach high school English at George Washington High School in the Bronx. Good grief, they actually have security guys at the doors there; have you ever heard of such a thing? Next, I got lucky—Carl's friend Betty Brown got me a temporary job filing at the offices of the New York Shakespeare Festival. Their offices are located in the Great Northern Hotel. My desk is in the hallway and Joe Papp thinks I'm a maid. I guess I won't be Ophelia by Tuesday, either.

I'm studying with Herbert Berghof at HB Studio. He doesn't think I'm a maid, but hasn't led me to believe he thinks I'm Maureen Stapleton, either. He obviously never saw my award-winning performance in Creston High School's glittering production of The Little Dog Laughed.

It's only a matter of time, kiddo ... I love it here. Have a glorious holiday.

Love,
Marcia

*P.S. I'm a woman who loves the subway. Call me crazy. ("But does the
subway love me back?" you ask.) I got on one morning during
hideous rush hour to fly off to my thrilling temp job at the
Chemical Bank, wearing, of course, one of my two size 22 black
skirts. It was big-time crowded; you know—you pick up your foot
and there's no place to put it back down. Well, I felt some rubbing,
thought I heard a zipper, and then thought, "Oh, it's just the near-
ness of New York's masses." Anyway, the car cleared at 34th, and
some woman who had been sitting there pointed to the back of my
skirt. So, always being a gal who loves to share, I marched into the
Chemical Bank and announced to a dozen people I didn't know,
"Can you believe it? Look at this skirt. Look what some pervert did
to me on the subway." I don't know what I expected in the way of
response, but they all looked like they'd rather have needles stuck
in their eyes then deal with me. I kept asking, "You don't think it's
a metaphor, do you? An omen of my life in the Big Apple?" Hey,
listen, hon—they can mug me, they can arrest me, they can come
on me—I ain't leaving. I love it here!*

New York was great. It just was the right path for me, because I
met such wonderful people, and I had such wonderful experiences. Some I got paid for, some I didn't.

I found an apartment at 92nd and Broadway for ninety dollars
a month. Cockroaches? We used to call them the June Taylor
Cockroaches. We'd walk through the door and they'd dance, "Doo-
doo, doo doo doo!" I'd never seen so many cockroaches in my life.

After about a year of rooming in Cockroach Heaven with my
friend Nancy Rhinehart, who had followed me out from Iowa, I
moved in with two other friends: Rosanna Huffman (she later married Richard Levinson, who created *Columbo*) and Carol Richards.
We all lived together in a floor-through brownstone on 76th Street
between Columbus and Amsterdam. It probably rents for thousands
of dollars now, but this was before they trendied up the neighborhood, when it was still very ethnic and kind of dangerous. Funky; I

liked it. I love the West Side; I don't understand living on the East Side at all.

Carol and Rosanna and I lived together while they were performing on Broadway in *Mame* and *Half a Sixpence*. Our rent was sixty dollars apiece. Then Rosanna and Richard got married and Carol moved out, and I lived with a gorgeous German showgirl for a while. She was the only person who ever called me a bitch—"You are ein *bitch*"—I can't remember why. I think my charms eluded her.

For my first job, I sold bedsheets at B. Altman's. They wanted me to be a buyer. "You're overqualified for a sales job," they told me. But I was going to be an actress. So after Altman's, I applied for a job typing scripts.

When I arrived to interview for the typing job, the woman in charge had a taxi waiting outside to take her to the loony bin. She said to this guy Joe Sicari, who was just typing there, "I'm going into the mental hospital; I need you to run my business for a few weeks."

Joe was just hilarious. He actually put in the ad, "Typist wanted: seven to ten fingers." He had a great sense of humor, so he hired me right off. I just said "hi" to Janet as she was leaving for the bin; in the years I worked for her, she went to the bin pretty regularly. But that's how I met Joe, who later became my son Mikey's godfather.

It was great work, because I was an enormously good typist, and you got paid ninety-five cents a page. I'm the person who typed the movie script for *Hello Dolly*. And of course in my twenties I never slept. So I could work at night doing improv at a club for free chili till four or five in the morning, and then go type scripts. It's such a small world—yesterday I heard David Duchovny talking about his father, who wrote a play called *The Trial of Lee Harvey Oswald*. I typed it.

Wits were what you needed in that city, or something more like instinct. Once, when I was typing at that all-night place, and I was on my way over to the West Side on the subway, some guy tried to follow me home. I got really scared at first, and then I thought, "Nobody wants to get involved with a nut. Maybe even your perverts won't want to come near you if you're crazy." So I started walking down the middle of the street singing "Some Enchanted Evening." After that, nobody ever came near me. They don't want to know from you if you're crazier than they are. The middle of the night. "Some Enchanted Evening."

I also tried my hand at substitute teaching in high school, but that was twenty-nine dollars a day and too hard. I was so gullible; I'd shout, "All right, come inside and write your name down." And then I'd call off their names to see if they were still there. You know, Mike Hunt, Dick Hurtz... "All right, Dick. Come on, I've had enough of this." The day I screamed *"Shutto uppo!"* to a group of Spanish-speaking students was my last on a teaching payroll.

Eventually I decided, "No, thanks. Typing is a much better deal for me." But I'm a worker. I was born with a Jay Leno-like prognostic jaw that used to show up about ten minutes before the rest of me— way, way out. And my teeth didn't go together, so there was no mastication; plus, they used to fall out like miniature bowling balls on the street. So there I was, starting a new life in New York City with about six teeth left, and thus began my dental saga.

My first dentist started by dropping an instrument down my throat and there's me gagging while he climbs on top of me to go after it. *Veerrrry* pleasant. And then he says, "Oh, sorry, and listen—this is the worst mouth I have ever seen, and I can't do a thing until you get this operation to give you a bite, and if you don't you'll end up with arthritis of the head."

So I had to get this operation. One of the first in the country where they moved your jawbone back and gave you a bite. This was my second year in New York, 1966, and of course I had no insurance, so I took three jobs to pay it off—twenty-five hundred dollars—a fortune to me. I worked at all these jobs, saved the money, and took the subway to the New York Polyclinic, alone, to have the surgery. They told me I'd have to be in the hospital for at least ten days. I said, "I've got no insurance; I ain't going to be here for no ten days." I went home in two. Young and fearless.

But I've always made enough money. Even if it was only thirty-five dollars, it was enough; what I needed at the time.

In college I had read Uta Hagen's book on acting, and when I came to New York I wanted to study with her. I auditioned, and she turned me down. She said, "Go study with somebody else for a while." And I thought, "Oh, gee, I should probably be upset—but all right, I'll do it." So I went down the list of acting teachers—eeny, meeny, miney—and I picked William Hickey, another well-known acting teacher. He was hilarious and talented and wildly eccentric; I think he's best known as the wheezing old guy in *Prizzi's Honor*.

Anyway, he let me in. I was dying for a class, and he was looking for a place to go and drink at night, so he found this nightclub on West 9th Street next to Trudy Heller's, a place called Hilly's. Hilly let us start an improv group there. Bill would be there in the morning while we were working out the improvs, but then decided it was way too early, and Jeremy Stevens took over (Jeremy is now producing *Everybody Loves Raymond*). Judd Hirsch was part of it, too. And Kent Broadhurst, who became one of my best friends and also helped me develop taste (I was missing the taste gene). The other members were Jimmy Manis and Bette Jane Raphael. It's where I met David Steinberg, Stiller and Meara, and Valerie Harper. It was a great time; we didn't get paid at all, but it was so much fun.

Then we got a producer who was also in some bizarre enterprise, fertilizer or something. These were not your run-of-the-mill producers. We ended up in a theater on 80th Street called, appropriately enough, Theater 80. Every once in a while I'll meet someone who saw us there. It was real improv; we ran for years. We called ourselves The Fourth Wall.

But if I had gotten what I wanted right away, which was to study with Uta, who knows what would have happened? Several years later I went back to the HB Studio, auditioned for her again, and this time she took me. But because I didn't get discouraged, I got to study with Bill and become friends with all those great talents.

A Lucky Break

One night, Dan Sullivan, who's now a big director, but who was then a second-string drama critic for the *New York Times*, literally looking for somewhere to come in out of the rain, stumbled into our show and saw me. We were never any Second City by a long shot, but we were good enough. And he came in and saw me do an improv, and he liked it and he wrote about it. You know, just like a human interest thing, in out of the storm. Front page. You could never have gotten him down there if you tried; it was sheer luck. And that's what I mean when I say, "You've got to have talent, but you've got to have tenacity and you've got to have luck." The last two are just as important as the first.

So he wrote it up, and a casting guy from *The Merv Griffin Show*, Paul Solomon, came down and saw me, liked me and hired me. I ended up doing seventy-five appearances on *The Merv Griffin Show*, every couple of weeks or so. Merv discovered so many people, much bigger names than me, like Lily Tomlin and Diane Keaton, but I definitely belong on the list.

Those were the days when they didn't do stand-up comedy, they did sit-down. My very first story on the show was about being attacked in the Dairy Queen (more on that later). It was all pretty exaggerated; I elaborated quite a bit to make it funnier, but it was all true. I never made anything up, and it was all pretty much put-down humor: "I went to a party and a guy asked me for my phone number. And at the end of the evening, he gave it back." That kind of thing.

Everybody encouraged me to do stand-up. But that was a moment when I was in the wrong place at the wrong time. Because as far as women stand-ups went, there were only Phyllis Diller and Joan Rivers. And in those days you couldn't get back into acting if you did it. Now, they give you a series if you bus tables at the Comedy Store. But then, no. And I didn't want to work on stage alone; I liked acting. I'm basically an improv gal. They'd call me at the last minute when somebody else couldn't make it.

Life and the Universe—
Two Things I'm Basically in Favor Of

They put Merv opposite Johnny Carson for about a year and a half. Eventually, he went back to his syndicated time slots, but one time during this period in L.A., they flew me out. It was one of those unbelievable chances—usually you just came on the show, you did your five minutes, and that was it. But that night he decided to bring all the guests out at once. I was on with all these starlets, real lookers: Donna Mills, an actress named Angel Tomkins, Anne Francis... I forget who else. There were five or six of us, and he said at the last minute, "Bring everybody out all at once." So everyone was very tense and very sincere, and they were talking about very esoteric things: life and the universe, et cetera. I hadn't said anything for the longest time, and finally Merv said, "What about you, Marcia?" and I said, "Oh, hon, I'm just trying to get somebody to take me bowling." So it turned out to be a real rave segment for me, and that's how I eventually got on *The Bob Newhart Show*.

I went from *The Merv Griffin Show* to the Newhart show. But along the way, I beat on about seven billion doors and showed up for about twenty thousand auditions, so it was no "overnight success." And Hilly's is where it started.

Somewhere in there, I was also in a production of *Dark of the Moon*. My friend Kent Broadhurst directed it, and his vision was that all the witches plus Witch Boy be nude. It was one of the first nude productions. I mean, *Hair* was before us, but I think they just had the one nude guy. We had several. (I myself was a townsperson and fully clothed.) It's amazing how fast you can get used to hanging out backstage with nude people. And they were not self-conscious at all and quite beautiful, but they had no pockets and were always mooching coins for the payphone.

Harvey Keitel was in it, quite intense even in his youth, and he got fired. Rue McClanahan was in it. *Dark of the Moon* is the fifth most staged play in the world, and that includes high school. It's so bad! It's awful. But Kent ran into this guy whose wife really liked the play, and her husband, Herb, was in the bowling alley business, and he produced it. But the theater fell in. It *fell in*, literally fell in. So we closed.

A Few Flings Are Flung

It was an unbelievably great time to be in New York. You could take a cab anywhere in the city for a dollar. After the show we'd go sit on the 59th Street Bridge with a picnic. I was in the Broadway show bowling league, and we used to bowl from midnight to three a.m. in Times Square. It was great, because after the shows were over, everybody stayed. Maybe they're still staying up all night—Joe Allen's, the Haystack, Jimmy Ray's, Downey's.

On the one hand I admire what's been done to 42nd Street recently, but it's a little Disney-ized. Back then, you could go to the movies all night long. You could get a pasta dinner for a dollar and a half. We'd eat and go to the movies and watch the sun come up on the Staten Island Ferry. I was in my twenties, and New York was livable and doable. I have nothing but fond memories; it was a great time. But was it romantic?

I had one boyfriend by the name of George, a comedian. I was listening to him in a club one night, and this guy next to me leans over and says, "He stole all his material from Lenny Bruce." But he was funny, and he started my long line of "boyfriends." His mother hated me. But I found out later he'd told her I was a defrocked nun. To say his apartment was filthy... you'd put things down and never see them again. A shoe would be sucked up into the vortex.

But there was something new this time; he was my first actual boyfriend and my first affair. I was twenty-five years old (always the late bloomer). He was funny at the movies—he'd do stuff like go out and then come back down the aisle in the middle of the movie with a blindfold over his eyes, calling my name: "Marcia? Marcia?!" "Over here, hon." That's another example of my never getting embarrassed.

The first one comes later. (I told you I was all over the place.) But then I got a job and George was mad about that. It was one of those things that just sort of ended. But I think of him fondly because it was kind of an important deal for me.

But mostly all I had was the occasional fling. Like with this other comic I met on the Griffin show—I'll call him Jerry. He had a wife, two mistresses and two girlfriends. And he was *funny*-looking. But he had a lot of something; I don't know what it was about him. His wife left him once, but he begged her to come back. He decided he'd rather cheat than date. I wonder if he's still alive. Those were the days long before it occurred to me that if you don't want somebody cheating on you, don't do it to somebody else. But in your twenties...

But perhaps you're wondering what came before all this hedonistic living. Hey, kids, it was the seventies. Now, as for how I wound up in New York in the first place...

2 don't look back

A Rocky Road, and I Don't Mean Ice Cream

D*on't look back, we're not going that way.*" That's what my father, Arthur "Poke" Wallace, told me right after flunking his real estate exam for the thirteenth time (he was nothing if not tenacious). It was a good piece of advice, but he had other reasons for wanting to turn his back on the past. As for me, if there's one thing I don't like, it's being told what to do. Or what *not* to do. So here I go, looking back...

I was born in Creston, a very small, very provincial town in Iowa. They called it Creston because it's the highest point between the Missouri and the Mississippi. That's our claim to fame. Besides me.

I personally have never met anybody who's had a perfect childhood. Some are better than others. Mine was a little on the rocky side, but I'll tell you something: it was never boring being Poke and Joann's oldest girl, and I had some wonderful times growing up in Creston. There have always been people there who wished me well and are proud of me to this day. Last summer my son Mikey wanted to see where I grew up, so we went back to visit. I said to him, "Honey, you've been to Disneyland; McKinley Lake might seem a little dinky." Well, he came, he saw, he loved it. "What a cool place." And seeing Creston again through my son's eyes, my little town never looked so beautiful.

Anyway, I was the oldest of three children born to Poke and Joann Wallace. Of all of us I was the most like my father, even though I looked like my mother. At least that's what people kept telling her. Which really pissed her off. Because she had always been told she was quite attractive, and nobody considered me attractive. So this was an ongoing struggle with us, every time she looked at me. More of that later.

I came into the world weighing twelve pounds, probably a portent of the conflict to come with my mother. My earliest memory is sitting in a high chair. Spitting food. At my mother.

World War II was still going on, and because my dad went into the navy when I was six months old, we lived with my grandma and granddaddy. That was my good fortune, because they were so great and I loved them so, and they loved me. My mother, meanwhile, went back to the "single life." Dancing in bars, partying—there was something to do every night, and she had free childcare. She was a real princess, an Iowa princess, if there was such a thing. Her parents idolized her, and she was *terribly* popular; always had tons of friends. And men... men just loved my mother. So when the war ended, she was very unhappy. By that time, she didn't want to be married to *no* poor guy, and she didn't want to have *no* kids.

Actually, they probably should never have gotten married. My father was just a really interesting, funny, goofy guy from the wrong side of the tracks. They had gone up to Hastings, Nebraska, and gotten married with no one in the family there, because my mother's parents disapproved; Dad was uneducated, unskilled, and a big drinker. He was also very handsome and very funny. I'm sure that was his appeal, because he looked a lot like Robert Mitchum or Victor Mature—one of those guys.

I remember the day my dad came home from the navy. I just thought he looked so handsome in his sailor uniform. He had been in the service for three and a half years. Joann had gone to visit him on leave, and managed to get pregnant again, with my sister Sherry. So Sherry was born when he was still gone, and my grandma took care of her, too. But now my father came home from the war for good. Years later, I found a letter that he wrote to his cousin when he was about to be discharged. He talked about how proud he was: "I'm so glad I could defend my country. I'll come back, and I'll raise my beautiful daughters and be with my beloved wife and be a good citizen..." It was an incredibly moving letter. And when he came back, it all blew up in his face. That's when my parents started their own war.

The Family Copes With Post-War Compression

The first thing that happened was that we moved out of my grandma's house—a swell old house—then moved to an apartment two houses away. A few months later we moved to something called the "GI units." These were actual barracks that had been shipped from some army camp somewhere—you know, those long Quonset huts. There were two of them facing each other, three apartments in each one. I think the rent must have been about twenty-five dollars a month. I can't begin to describe how small they were; the bedrooms weren't much bigger than an average bathroom. And they were *tacky*. They even had a pot-bellied stove. Everybody had at least three or four kids in each one of these. It was great for me and my sister, but my mother was *not* happy.

So there my parents were, faced with the truth of a marriage that shouldn't have happened. She didn't want to be a wife or a mom. She was crabby at being forced out of her parents' home, crabby about suddenly finding herself responsible for two little girls, and crabby about being married to a guy with no skills and a head injury from the war.

I guess they didn't get divorced because he loved her so much. I guess she loved him, too, on some level. And by this time, her parents figured, "You made your bed; you have to lie in it." Besides, this was the fifties. Things were different in the fifties. There was a funny story that my parents used to love to tell: they took me to a bar by the name of Beda's in my little carrier case when I was six months old, and they put me behind the bar, and they got drunk and they left me there all night. I stayed there all night, six months old, behind the bar at Beda's. Maybe it wasn't all night; maybe they woke up around four. But the point is, you tell that story today, you're in jail for child abuse. But they used to *regale* people with that story, how funny it was. And, you know, it's not *un*funny.

Anyway, what helped me in those days was that I was very, very close to my mother's parents, Madge and Cully. My grandfather sold hogs; my grandmother was a housewife. I always think how odd it is that a woman so unlike me—she had so much class and dignity, she was so soft-spoken and so lovely—was the only person who loved me unconditionally back then. That's the best of all, isn't it? When they look at you and you're nothing like them, and they like you anyway. She taught me to read, she taught me to drive; I remember sitting on her lap at great length. And the whole family—they were all so incredibly low-key. I used to do this imitation of my mother laughing hysterically:

Ha.

Ha.

Ha.

I'm much more of a Wallace. My father's side of the family is funny, angry, impulsive. The Wallace guys and gals are very *loud*. We laugh a lot, we talk a lot, and everybody's entitled to our opinion. I don't remember that my father, who talked about everything, ever mentioned his parents. Except once. He said his mother was a saint, and she just worked so hard on that farm it killed her. She died feeding the chickens when she was about fifty-five.

I'm really grateful I had those early years when I got a lot of attention and a lot of positive regard and love from my grandma. My grandpa, too, but mostly my grandma. Because when my father came back and we moved out, the trouble started.

A Reason Not to Have Children: It Creates Parents

The four of us moved into a cramped apartment two houses down from my grandparents. I kept leaving that new place and walking back to my grandma's house because that was the only place I'd ever lived, and I just loved them so. And my mother didn't want to be where she was, and I always drove her crazy. I tried to get her to tell me later on what it was about me that drove her so crazy, but she never could say. Anyway, I would go back to my grandparents, and my mother would start her thing about, "We can't let her go down there..." She baited my father, baited him and baited him until he was crazy.

I remember this one time when I was about four, him coming down to pick me up and him being "tense." I sensed a great deal of tension. And he was very big, he was about six foot three; he took me by the hand, he walked me the half block back to our apartment, walked me inside, picked me up and threw me against the wall. This kind of thing makes you real pragmatic real fast. There were a lot of "uh-ohs" from age four up. "Uh-oh, here it comes. Uh-oh!" That alarm came in real handy.

My father had no impulse control; he always took it out on the kids. Because he hit my mother once and she left him. And he couldn't risk that, because he just loved her.

That's one of the reasons I hate whistling so much, because he used to whistle around the house when he was trying to not hit us. It never quite worked. I've been known to jump out of cabs when somebody starts whistling.

It's clear to me now it wasn't just me. My mother pretty much summed it up by saying, "I notice you talk to Mikey a lot. We didn't do that in my day." And that is for sure. The fifties were different. Children were seen and not heard. Very few rights. And if people were under pressure, they often hit their children. But there's no excuse for beating children.

Where was my mother in this? Well, she'd never get mad. She'd just stand around to make sure it wasn't *really* going to hurt, and she'd murmur, "Arthur, the neighbors." She was really something. She didn't have any career aspirations herself; bourbon and coke and Pall Malls were my mom's ambition. Oh, and to be married to a rich guy. She used to work in the sundries store with my dad; she was hilarious. She'd come up and sit on the stool. And a guy would come in and say, "I'd like a malt."

And she'd say, "I'm sorry, I don't make malts. It hurts my arm."

"But up on the menu it says 'malts.' I'd like a malt."

"I don't make malts. *Arthur, someone wants a malt!* Can't scoop—it hurts my arm."

The older I got and the fatter I got, the more my mother couldn't stand it. I used to walk into the room, and you'd actually see her upper lip curl with contempt. That's how much she hated the way I looked. And of course, the less I was like her and the more weight I gained, the more people said, "Marcia looks just like you." Oh, it used to drive her crazy.

She was a piece of work, my mother. But I'll tell you something: I have nothing but warm feelings about her. We resolved a lot of things, she and I, before she died, because people do the best they can. It's so amazing, that observation. All of us can get in touch with something our parents did to us when we were six, but it's a lot fuzzier when we have to say what we're doing to *our* children, what we did yesterday that was potentially harmful. It's not easy; you're not nearly so clear on that.

Look, smacking kids is wrong and it doesn't work, but now that I'm a parent I certainly understand the impulse. I don't think there's a parent alive who, if they're being honest, doesn't understand child abuse. You just don't do it; you walk out of the room if you have to, something I do often as a parent. I leave the room; sometimes I leave the house, and occasionally I want to leave town. So I try not to sit in judgment anymore on parents—including my own—unless they're just horrible, because it's just too damn hard to be one.

Now, about my father: he barely made it through the ninth

grade, but he was a real entrepreneur, always coming up with wild new ideas. He could talk people into anything. When he noticed that nobody ever engraved anything on the back of a headstone, he talked some guy into sharing his: "Hey, listen, you're not gonna use the back of that thing, are you? That's wasted space, there." And before the guy could answer, my dad went out and had his name chiseled on the back. It's probably the only double-sided gravestone in the world.

He was like nobody else I've ever met. Beatings aside, he's given me a couple of things that have come in awfully handy as I've approached the tough challenges of my life, and those are tenacity and a sense of humor. I got both of those from my dad. He was an alcoholic, and it's a shame he never used the AA program, because he would have been such an inspiration to other people. He was what they call a "dry alcoholic"; he'd go on periodic binges. But even without the binges, he was a character, truly one of a kind.

I tell everyone I can never be embarrassed, because if you had my dad for a father, you got it out of the way early. In the fifth grade, my mother got mad because I wore her shoes to school. So my dad came to school and burst into the classroom, yelling, "Gimme them shoes!" Yanked them off my feet. And he left. And there I was, barefoot. Runner-up on the embarrassment meter would be the time my father pulled me aside at the store for one of our intimate father-daughter chats. It seems that as I approached puberty I had developed an unfortunate odor, and nobody knew what to say. Well, Poke did, and here's what he said: "Marsh, here's the deal: you stink!"

But like I said, the upside to that is that nothing embarrasses me. Nothing. I couldn't care less what you do. And that's not a bad lesson. Because the thing about being raised in the Midwest is, you care very much about what people think and what people say—a big waste of time, if you ask me.

On the other hand, the great thing about growing up in a small town in the fifties was the freedom, which kids today will never understand. I mean, to walk out the door and do whatever you want.

I wouldn't say I loved being unpopular (until I discovered

humor), but I learned to be self-motivated and I used to do a lot of things on my own. I was a voracious reader. I used to go out and swim by myself. It all sounds kind of sad, but if you learn to be alone and to motivate yourself, this is only a good thing.

My mother was a flawed parent, no question about it, and she didn't like me much, certainly not in my formative years. But that didn't seem so terrible to me. What *did* was that no one would admit what was going on. To this day, people don't want to admit that it's possible for a mother not to like her child. But it happens. It happened to me, and I'm sure I'm not the only one. For whatever reason; I mean, it's a loaded relationship to begin with. I tried to work on it, and I kept trying to get her to talk about it: "When you said, 'I don't love you, and no one will ever love you, you're too fat,' did you really mean that?" I asked my mother that question on the phone when I was about twenty-five. My sister said my mother dropped the phone, ran out of the house, put her fingers in her ears and started humming hysterically. So much for open dialogue!

I may have looked like my mother, but we couldn't have been less alike. I was loud and messy; she was soft-spoken and real neat. I've always enjoyed swearing; I only heard her say two dirty words in her life, both inspired by me. The first time was this: I believed in Santa Claus for so long that she finally said to me, "You're thirteen, you're embarrassing me; there's no fucking Santa Claus." Then, three years later, the mother of a friend called and told my mother to keep me away from her daughter as I was a bad influence, which was hilarious since my friend could have taught *me* plenty; in fact, almost everyone could have taught me plenty in those days. But my mother actually stood up for me. Before she slammed the phone down she said: "And furthermore . . . bullshit!" I was thrilled.

My parents were hilarious in later years when I was really angry and expressing some feelings for the first time. My father used to say, "Well, your mother didn't like you. That's your problem; your mother didn't like you." Then I'd go to my mother, and my mother would say, "Well, your father beat you up." Both of those things were true, but oddly enough, my father, for all of his real anger and lack of control, would *try* to calm himself down so he wouldn't hit us. Gotta give him credit for trying.

But to this very day I still can't eat "family" meals. I'm a grown woman, and I still can't sit at a table and eat a meal in my own house. I can go to restaurants; I can go to other people's houses. But trapped in that breakfast nook, in the fifties, in that house at 1010 N. Division... it was one of those booths you couldn't get out of. I sat next to my mother, Sherry sat next to my dad, and my mother started drinking, and I guess the blood-sugar hit, and the fights started. Food was thrown and children were hit. I think I found a fourteen-year-old chicken bone down in the basement once. It was just a terrible time, and my sister—my sister still won't eat dinner till midnight, and then only in her room.

Not only were my eating habits affected by all this, but so was my sleep. When I was thirty-five and in the hospital, my friend Claudia Newcom came to see me and said, "Marcia, put your head down on your pillow." I said, "It is." She said, "No, it's not. Here..." She came over and pushed my head down about three or four inches, and I realized that up till then I had been sleeping with my head perched on top of the pillow, ever ready. Talk about your sore necks.

I can trace this back to those pesky nights when my dad would barge in the room and wake us up to scream or hit us. Once, when my sister's friends had toilet-papered the front yard, I was sound asleep, and the next thing I knew I was up a tree at three a.m. removing toilet paper. And it wasn't even *my* friends who did it. At that time, I didn't even have enough friends to TP a bush, let alone a tree.

As I said, my mother genuinely did not like me. A lot of it was tied up with appearances, and appearances are important in small towns, certainly in the Midwest anyway. How you look is much more important than who you *are*. As long as it *looks* right, as long as it *looks* presentable, it doesn't matter if there's a kind of undertow going on. My sister used to say, "Why don't you just do what I do, suck up?" I don't think she said "suck up" in those days, but she was always crying, "Oh, Mommy, Daddy! Oh, Mommy, Daddy! Oh, Mommy, Daddy! Sorry!"

My sister has given me some very good advice, but according to everybody who was there, I used to just stare at them. I used to stare people down. Which probably got me hit an awful lot. And, well, Poke had to do *something* with his anger, with how his life had gone to hell, and how nothing he did worked out.

I was a very good student, and I remember being in the second grade and drawing a picture of a person with a red face. That's a sure sign of anger, and today anybody would follow up on it. But in those days, individual expression was not encouraged. I remember the teacher saying, "You cannot draw a red face on the little girl." When I asked why, she said, "You can't do it; we don't have red faces." Well, I don't think I said, "What do you care?" But I do remember trying to stick to my guns on this. She wore me down and made me do it again. It was that sort of thing that made it all so hard. It was that era, so tranquil and so boring, and everything was so not what it appeared.

The Others

You might have thought with all of this that I was jealous of other, happier kids. I really wasn't, and I wonder why. I think I'm very fortunate in this. Of all the flaws I have, and I have plenty, I've never been a person who was unduly envious or jealous, because if I was going to be jealous of other people, I'd never get out of bed. My fight has always been with myself, trying to see how I could do it better.

Besides my grandparents, I loved my Auntie Cecilia a great deal. She's been such a positive force in my life. She is my father's sister and has his courage and humor without his darker side. I adore her.

Likewise I adore my Uncle Jimmy. His wife, Marge, is pretty cool, too. He's my mother's brother, and he was a doctor — *my* doctor. It was okay to do that in those days. Uncle Jimmy worked really hard all week. He even made house calls day and night, so he tended to unwind by playing golf on Thursday afternoons, and was known to have a few drinks. One day he got on a rant about Kennedy. He was a true conservative and just hated JFK. He decided to call the White House and give him a piece of his mind. Of course he couldn't get through. So he said, after several more drinks, "Hell, it's probably easier to get a hold of goddamn Khrushchev." So he placed a call to the Kremlin. No luck, and he went home. At four a.m., the phone rang and it was—guess who?—one of Nikita's boys returning the call. My Uncle Jimmy, who was not feeling great at that time, muttered, "Dr. Gault is dead," and hung up. I love that story.

When I had all those injuries from my father—he broke my nose, my collarbone—and I always wondered if Uncle Jimmy guessed what was going on. I think they all did, but nobody did anything about it. Not even my grandparents.

I used to go to school with black eyes. It's not like I tried to hide it. People used to say, "What happened to your nose?" And I would say, "My father hit me!" And they'd get real busy looking at their shoes; nobody said a word. Believe me, there was plenty going on beside my stuff. We all knew about a friend of mine—her father sexually abused several of her friends. Nobody said a word. No one cared. Or if they did, they were too scared to do anything. I don't remember thinking that any of this was out of the ordinary. The frustration for me was that I wanted to talk to other people about this stuff and nobody wanted to do that. It was a "small-talk" decade, and there I was this kid who wanted to talk personal.

My grandparents hadn't wanted my mother to marry my dad, but eventually they came to accept him, because he was a good provider—for a guy with no education. He never made more than five or eight thousand dollars a year, but that was enough.

My dad had a sundries store. First it was Bradley Drug, but when the pharmacist died off, my dad didn't want to hire a new one, so it became Wallace Sundries. He hired my sister and me and my Aunt Cecilia to work there. Without pay, of course. He was building the infamous "Midwestern work ethic," and naturally he believed it was a rare treat for all of us to work at Wallace Sundries, Home of the

Famous Ham Sandwich. Sherry was much better at it than I was. I didn't get paid, and still I got fired nine times. Sometimes he'd just call up and say, "Be gone by the time I get there." Once he fired me while he was cutting the ham, and he was so worked up, he held the knife upside down, and—oh, my—he bled all over the ham. I guess I was a goner for good the day he ran into a friend of mine on the street and complimented her on her nice scarf, and she said, "Oh, thanks. I was just in the store and Marcia gave it to me." I never did well in retail. Wallace Sundries was where, eventually, when we were grown up, my dad would sell every present Sherry and I sent him. When finally we got clever and had things engraved, we'd find him chipping away at them. "Oh, damn, Marcia, it fell off! Look at that—fell right off." And next thing you know it'd be in the store, for sale on the shelf there. He was proud of Wallace Sundries; it was all he wanted to do. He was open late at night on Sundays and made a fortune for a couple of years, and then, of course the K-Marts came to town, the malls, the places you could go and get a roll of film a lot cheaper on Sunday. But for a while he did it when nobody else did it. He had a tremendous work ethic.

I was always looking for a mother elsewhere. There was a woman across from us in one of the barracks by the name of Lois. She was married to a guy named Howard. (His mother was one of those women in town who fitted people for bras. I think there were those women in all those stores where you'd go in to get a bra and they'd help you get the right size and feel you up—every town had one of those.) Anyway, Lois had a little girl named Barbie. Barbie was a beautiful kid with brown curls, and Lois worshipped her; everybody did. Barbie was sweet and she was lovely and you couldn't not like her. One night we were all going to have a barbecue out at McKinley Park, all of us from the units. Everybody went, and Barbie ate and then she ran to the swings. Well, she fell out of the swings and she broke her arm and they took her to the hospital.

A Death in the Family

I couldn't sleep all that night, and I woke up knowing something was wrong. I was only about seven. I looked out; my bed was right next to the window. Ordinarily, we had to go to bed year-round, including the summer, at six o'clock, so my mother could start having a little "downtime." So I spent a lot of time looking out that window. And I kept looking out that window to see where Lois and Howard's car was, because it wasn't there.

Finally it was morning, and I got up and I heard that Barbie, the beautiful Barbie, had died the night before. This story has haunted me forever. As I look back almost fifty years, I'm not quite sure exactly what happened, but Barbie did die and this is my memory, however flawed, of that horrible night: when she broke her arm, they took her to the hospital. The doctor on call came in, and my Uncle Jimmy, a new young doctor just out of medical school, was also there that night. They discussed pumping her stomach, but Lois couldn't bear Barbie's crying and pain and strongly urged them to put her under and set her arm.

Of course, they should not have done that. She choked on a piece of chicken and died. I always heard that my Uncle Jimmy was so upset he was asked to leave the operating room. He had thought her stomach should be pumped before they gave her the anesthetic, but he was overruled. My Aunt Marge told me all this. She had just given birth and was in the hospital that night.

Prior to that time, I used to go to Lois's door. My image of myself as a kid was just looking through screen doors, being on the outside, looking in a screen door at the good stuff going on inside. I was always on the inside looking out or the outside looking in. I got on a lot of people's nerves back then, but Lois always smiled and invited me in. And after my mother and her curling lip, whenever somebody saw me and their face lit up, it just meant the world to me. I'm still that way. I have a thing about faces; I think I overreact a bit.

Anyway, they had a funeral for Barbie, and they had a viewing.

That's what they did in the fifties; at least, the Catholics did. My god, my uncle Frank died, and his casket was in the living room. I mean, there was Uncle Frank, right next to the ham. I found it very creepy, but wakes and viewing were very big in the Midwest. Very, very big. People always used to say, "Oh, doesn't he look so lifelike?" (Uh, no, he looks *dead.*) So there was Barbie, dead. I had never seen a dead person before, and she looked all puffy from, you know, the clamps, probably, trying to hold her mouth open, and it was really awful. But I thought, "Now *I* can be Lois's daughter." Even though she had two other children who were just babies, somehow I thought maybe if I was good enough—I knew I wasn't cute enough—but if I was *good* enough, maybe I could be her daughter and replace Barbie. And then I thought, "Oh, dear, does that mean I'm glad she's dead?" It was a horrible tangle of feelings, and a very, very important event in my life, one that I still haven't quite sorted out. I can still see that little girl in her coffin.

Lois was inconsolable and blamed herself after Barbie died. I would go over there and try to amuse her, try to make her feel better, but I was just a seven-year-old dippy kid, and sometimes she was so depressed she wouldn't let me in. Anyway, one night, she went out, drove out to the cemetery and had some sort of freak accident. I'm still not quite sure what happened, or even if anybody knows for sure. She fell, hit her back or her neck, and became paralyzed. (Hello— isn't this a wonderful story?) So now she's in a wheelchair and her daughter is dead.

And then about five years down the line, while she was para- lyzed, she got pregnant again and she had a daughter she named Becky. Becky was a wonderful girl, and Lois was still a wonderful mother to those kids. My Uncle Jimmy was her doctor the rest of her life. We had moved by this time, but I always stayed in touch with her, and she was always extremely proud of me. She died when she was in her mid-sixties, and it was all amazing, because she shouldn't have been able to give birth to that baby, and with her injury she shouldn't have lived that long a life. It's one of those mythical, gothic stories from small towns all around the country, and it's one that certainly affected me. Because I wanted her to be my mother.

A Life in the Family

When I was thirteen, my mother got pregnant again. I remember being in the car with my sister, who was eleven, and she said, "Well, I got news for you, girls. You're going to have a brother or sister."
"Oh! Oh! Oh! When?"

"Yeah, well, in October." Oh, she was not happy. And she smoked and drank her way through that pregnancy, just like she did through all the others. Imagine if she *hadn't* smoked or drunk. I weighed twelve pounds. My sister weighed ten, and my brother weighed eight.

My dad was beside himself with joy. He almost fell down the elevator shaft the night Jimmy was born. It's interesting that to this day, my brother will never get over the loss of his dad. He was the best dad in the world to my brother. He was forty-five, though, by the time my brother was born. And he pretty much took over.

One of the closest times I had with my dad was taking care of Jimmy. My brother was colicky and had seizures—those fever seizures that stop automatically when you're about four—where it's like the crib is being shaken by six grown people. A hundred and five, a hundred and six degrees, and you start having convulsions. It would happen in the middle of the night. It was just awful, and my dad and I would take turns holding him. My mother was sleeping. I shouldn't have been up, you know, walking that baby with my dad. But I was thrilled to see that baby, just thrilled to see him. I took him everywhere with me, and it just fit right into my unpopular mode. He was five when I went away to college.

Jimmy just loved my dad, and my dad was great with him. Talked to him, played golf with him, helped him get jobs, encouraged him—as awful as he was with us girls, that's how great he was with Jim. Maybe if you have kids later? Maybe if he'd only had boys? Who knows.

My mother wasn't all that interested. So it was fine that I was acting like his mother. And then later on I remember he used to blackmail Sherry and me, because I'd find my Christmas presents and open them. He charged me a quarter not to tell for every present I opened. He had a real business going there.

I never really saw him much after I left for college. But those first five years I remember taking him by myself out into the woods, and he'd be on a blanket, or I'd take him on my bike in the little basket. It just made me feel better. Those early puberty years were just so desolate for me. I looked so damned old, and I didn't have any friends. I hadn't discovered humor yet, like I did later in high school when everybody finally perked up and took notice. Now, nobody was talking to me, nobody was interested in me, and I was getting beaten up at home, so when my brother came along, it was like a present. I gladly got up and walked him at night. I took care of him all the time. As I say, I left home when he was five, and we never again lived in the same town. Now he's a pharmacist and lives with his family in Davenport, Iowa, but I will always remember those times when he was a little boy.

3 don't look back

Fast Times at the Dairy Queen

Now, I was Catholic in the fire-and-brimstone days of the fifties. It's gotten much more life-affirming, the Catholic church, and much more upbeat. But in the fifties there were two things to look out for: the Commies and hell; we're all going to hell unless the Commies get us first. When I was a teenager, the priest used to ask me, "What about sex?" I would say, "I haven't had sex." And he'd say, "I know you kids. It's okay. You've got to tell me; you've got to make a full, complete confession."

One day he actually said to me: "I know all about you kids. Listen, you play ball with me, I'll play ball with you." And that was like, "Waiter? Check, please," because I hadn't had sex; hadn't even thought about it. And by the time I was having sex, I wouldn't have confessed it anyway. So that was pretty much it for me. But the very first time I went to confession, I wrote down all my sins, put my name on the paper, and lost it in the church. Somebody returned this to my mother. So my father mortified me, and I mortified my mother. Everything I did was too big, too much.

Religious Experiences

My mother had long ago given up the Church. In fact, she was

29

Catholic for about twenty minutes. But my father insisted that we go to church through high school, and we were very close to our Aunt Cecilia, who was wildly religious; she went to Mass every day. So there we were in Catechism with this grim, grim old, smelly old priest from the fifties. And of course every Good Friday from twelve to three, which are the hours when our blessed Lord died on the cross. And we had to fast. In high heels and garter belts. I got *sooo* hungry and *sooo* dizzy and my damn knees hurt and once or twice I even keeled over and came to with the dreaded Monsignor Stoll glaring down at me.

"Uh, I got dizzy."

"Dizzy? Dizzy? You think Jesus ever got dizzy?"

"Well, possibly, if I could just have a cracker…"

"Cracker? *Cracker*? Nobody gave Jesus a cracker, you miserable excuse for a Catholic."

Quite a charmer, wasn't he? You had to give money to the church, or else you were going to hell. (Actually, just about everything you did sent you straight to hell.) This priest taught catechism, which I had to start at age seven; this meant I couldn't go to Saturday afternoon movies any more, so I was not happy about that.

It also became clear to me pretty early on that my prayers were not working out. I don't think it made me mad so much as it made me think, "Well, I'm going to try another approach here." And I think that's what made me stop wanting to look outside myself for spiritual answers, and led me eventually to Eastern religion and to Buddhism. Because that whole concept of heaven and hell, of do what you want all week and then on Sunday throw yourself on the mercy of the church and it's all undone? Well, it just seemed wildly arbitrary and unfair to me. I've always had a thing about "unfair." I try not to let it be an issue, because you could spend a lot of time being upset about how unfair life is. I mean, it's not my style to say "That's not fair" where something concerns *me*. But when I look outside myself and see the terrible things that go on, it steams me.

Anyway, I didn't see that religion ever caused people to treat each other better. I was from a family in a town that was totally white, where people weren't crazy about anyone who wasn't like them. I don't think anyone had malice. I don't think anyone would have, given the chance, burned any crosses or anything, but clearly there were some very pejorative words used about minorities. Most people were, at least subliminally, prejudiced at that time, even my beloved grandparents. I don't know why I didn't have any prejudice, because I certainly didn't grow up with anybody who didn't look like me, but I've never had a problem accepting people for who they are. We had one black family in town, and the dad shined shoes at the train station. (So much for Affirmative Action.) I used to wonder, "What is it like being the only black family in town?" They had a daughter (who didn't date, of course). And everybody was nice enough, but it must have been so lonely and isolating. I experienced something similar, on a much smaller scale, decades later when my house burned and I ended up living in the Koreatown section of Los Angeles for six months. I was the only Caucasian on my block, and, boy, did I feel weird and out of place. Anyway, my dad went through his whole life calling black men "boy." And I'd say, "They're going to beat the hell out of you, Dad." And he'd say, "Oh, no. Hell, no, they like me."

And maybe because they sensed no real malice in him, no one ever did. I mean he was just goofy.

My Life As a Crash Test Dummy

I was clumsy, *extremely* clumsy, as a child. When I was seven, we got a community bicycle, my sister and I. I thought I knew how to ride it, but I went around the corner and was coming back down the hill near the units when I realized I didn't know where the brakes were! My mother and my sister were outside, waving at me. They thought I was laughing, but I was yelling, "Help! I can't stop it!" So, on my bike, I raced across the street, up into a yard. This woman is sitting on her front porch. She has a little teeny stoop. She gets up, opens the front door, I drive the bike in and crash into her sofa. So it seems to me, because I'd get impulsive and do things without thinking them out first, I always had to learn my lessons the hard way.

In terms of sex education in those days, there was none. I remember I experienced the first fire in my loins when I was a little girl and I saw Roy Rogers. He made me feel queasy. Oh, I loved that Roy; I loved that Roy. And I remember feeling a lot of those feelings as a very little girl, and kissing a lot of neighbor boys, and being very much in touch with my body. Then the beatings started. And I developed way too soon. It made me wildly uncomfortable; I got lots of weird looks. So I just started eating. Hell, I just ate and ate and ate and ate. I looked like a grown woman when I was about ten or eleven years old. Salesmen would come to the door and ask if my husband was home. I said, "I'm nine!"

Now, I know a lot of people didn't attempt to talk about sex education back then. People didn't talk about anything. Anyway, my father, outrageous as ever, took it upon himself to teach me about sex. He was unflappable. Oh, he mortified me again and again. My sister was real cute and real popular from a very young age. Whenever she was with a boy, my father would lurk in the bushes and jump out and practically give them a heart attack. Then he would try to talk the boy into asking me out.

Sex Ed the Fifties Way

I never had a date in high school. Except once. The day before the junior prom, a guy who didn't date either asked me to the prom. I called my grandma and told her and she was so happy, she drove me all the way to Des Moines the very next day to get me a prom dress at Younkers. I loved my grandma. But getting back to my sex education—my father sat me down and said (and this is a direct quote), "Sooner or later, someone's going to try to get in your pants."

Well, didn't this just paint a romantic picture of love and sex? So that was pretty much it. It's amazing what I didn't know. I was certainly not sexually active; I was a virgin into adulthood. My freshman year in college, I had a roommate by the name of Pixie. She was awfully cute and perky, and she was having quite an intense relationship of a sexual nature with her boyfriend, and she used to talk about it all the time. I was just caught up like crazy, soaking this up; she was saying something that sounded like a bad romance novel, and then she said: "And he put it in—"

"Ew!" I said. *"It goes inside?!"* Now, I was seventeen years old. How in the world I could have gotten to be seventeen years old and not know there was penetration? But somehow... I don't know what I thought, if I thought about it. It's just that after those earliest urges for Roy Rogers, I pretty much went into a *long* latent period, covered by a lot of fat, and sublimated through humor, and I guess I thought men and women just sort of rubbed together and the sperm just sort of jumped across; I don't know. I imagine you could grow up with a lot of misconceptions about sex, which is why my son Mikey talks at great length about it, probably giving me more information than I need.

Binge Living

When my father couldn't think of what to call something, he used to call it a tit. So when he wanted you to turn off the lights or pull the chain on the fans, he'd say, "Pull that tit behind you there," in front of everyone. The man was a lunatic.

My favorite story about my dad took place in Chicago. He used to go there on an occasional bender. My mother went with him at first, but she said he was no fun, and god knows the woman wanted to have fun. She said he used to drink a bottle, throw up, pass out, wake up, and here we go again. Actually, she may be right on this one; it doesn't sound like a million laughs. So he started going alone for a few days. He'd binge, check himself into the hospital at the end of the binge, sober up and then come home.

After years of this ritual, his doctor in Chicago died, so the next time, he didn't come home when expected. It seems he had fallen down the steps at Union Station. (Ever picturesque, he later told the local newspaper his cab had been carjacked.) He was missing for days. Finally we heard from a Chicago hospital, "Please come immediately." We all flew to Chicago, where the doctors pulled us aside and said in hushed tones, "We're afraid there's been brain damage." So we went in, talked to him for a while, came out and told the doctors, "Nope, that's Poke." Luckily I found the forty-two condoms in his suitcase before my mother did. And I wonder where I got my optimism; what a guy. I don't think he finished a sentence after 1958, but he was a genuinely interesting person. And he didn't pass through unnoticed; not a lot of us can say that.

Some Men Just Love a Woman in Uniform

My first story on Merv Griffin—what my friend Charlie Cilona used to describe as my bent for turning tragedy into comedy—was how I was attacked while working at the Dairy Queen, and it's a true story. There I was in my Dacron uniform, age fourteen, and the guy I was working for, some old guy, said, "Come into the back with me; I want to show you something." So we're in the back, and he says, "We've got to change the milk cans in the freezer." The next thing I know, he closes the door and starts grabbing my clothes and my breasts and sticking his tongue in my mouth and all that. But he was old, and had a heart condition, so he kept having to stop and wheeze! I thought, "This is some sort of a bad joke here." I was so big; and I was only fourteen!

Fourteen. But after that happened, I *really* started to gain weight. I think it's true what they say about child abuse, weight and food. I developed very early; if I had never been fat, I would have had a great figure because I was very developed. But I didn't ever have a sense of myself. I felt so vulnerable; people looked at me funny, so I protected myself, and I gained weight. When I told my mother about this Dairy Queen incident—I told several people about it, I never kept anything to myself—my mother said, "You know, I know his wife, so let's just not mention it." But this was not unusual, not in the fifties. Denial ruled.

I used to baby-sit for this family across town, and every time Sherry or I would go over there, the father would say, "Come here; I want to show you something about the baby." And he'd get me in a room with the baby, and then he'd whip out his penis. I wanted to say, "Put that *away!*" Sometimes they'd come home together, him and his wife, and it would still be out. And I'd think, "Doesn't she *notice* that it's *out?* Is nobody ever going to tell him to put that *away?*"

If he did it to us, he probably did it to everybody. But my mother didn't want to know about it. There was smarmy, ugly stuff going on all the time, and nobody wanted to talk about it, and nobody wanted to get involved. Except me. I was always in somebody's face wanting to talk personal, and this was the fifties, for god's sake; nobody talked about scary stuff. And there was me talking about my dad hitting me, and the guy molesting me, and of course everybody was wildly uncomfortable. No wonder people hated to see me coming. (My best friend Brett once said to me when I was giving her what she referred to as "the look," "Well, your father was right. He should have hit you more.") I did not, however, have the nerve to tell anyone about the guy who kept whipping his penis out when I went to baby-sit, probably because I'd never seen one before. When I think back on all those times I always wish I'd said, "*Oh, my—that looks just like a penis, only smaller.*"

Getting My Act Together

I didn't have many friends until high school, when I discovered humor. Self-deprecating humor. I started putting myself down, and the kids would laugh and laugh. That's why I loved high school; I finally figured out how to be popular. There was even a guy who told me later that he wanted to ask me out, but he didn't have the guts; people would have made fun. Because I was, you know, fat, and not the kind of girl guys asked out. But I look back now, and I wasn't nearly as unattractive as I felt or thought I was. Then again, a lot of the prettier girls got pregnant, or married right out of high school, and that was the end of that. So maybe I was lucky, because I always thought, "I've got to get out of here or I'll never have a life."

I took inventory, trying to figure out what I had going for myself growing up in Iowa that I could parlay into an interesting life, because it had already been made very clear to me that I wasn't beautiful. I was smart, but nobody knew it, and I had a couple of things that have come in awfully handy: tenacity and a sense of humor, both of which, as I said, I got from my dad.

If I'd been born twenty years later I probably would have ended up homeless on Hollywood Boulevard; but you didn't run away from home in my day. I left, though. When I was seventeen years old. But I'd started feeling I had to get out back when I was eight or nine. Those were grim times; my mother so unhappy with her life, she desperately wanted to have more and be more. But I didn't do it to her! It wasn't my fault! Even then I knew that.

In high school I wanted to be a journalist, but my journalism teacher actually said to me, "Sweetie, you have no nose for news." She was right. The thought of going out and shoving microphones in people's faces—oh, no. Ugh! So I tried out for the school play instead, something called *The Little Dog Laughed*, and I got a good part. And *then* I won Best Supporting Actress. After that play there were others, and I was funny in all of them. The humor was at my expense, of course, but I loved it because I was suddenly popular.

That same journalism teacher began to encourage me to go into drama. She said, "I'm telling you, you could make it in the theater." She was a great teacher—Darlene Green. She suggested (because she was the only mentor I had, the only one who was giving me advice in anything, and she liked me, so I figured she wouldn't steer me wrong), "Why don't you go to a small college on a scholarship, and then you can always transfer?" Nobody else ever asked me where I was going to college, or *if* I was going to college, or what did I want. I was on my own, always. I filled out all the forms, applied and got accepted to Parson's College in Fairfield, Iowa. With a full scholarship. Nobody in my family ever expected me to do much. They were wrong.

Parson's College was a school that was kind of famous in the sixties. It was on the cover of *Life* magazine, referred to as "Flunk Out U." It was started by a guy named Millard Roberts. He bought up this old Presbyterian college, and he took rich kids who flunked out of Ivy League universities. He said, "Come to us." So the college wound up with tons of money. They had a lot of doctoral programs, and the third highest paid faculty in the country after Harvard and the University of Chicago. Of course, nothing was expected of anybody back then except keg parties, so there were freshmen who had been there for eons.

But they had a really wonderful summer drama program. There was a lot of money in the till, so they would bring in B-movie stars like Virginia Mayo and Pat O'Brien, and they brought in people from the faculty of Carnegie Tech. It was called the Parsons Summer Festival, and it was great. I was in plays with all these terrific people. And I met a wonderful family there, the Lambs—they became sort of a surrogate family to me. And I heard that applause and I never turned back. I decided I didn't want to transfer, and I was really starting to get happy. I think my parents actually even came to see some of the shows. I was getting so much encouragement, and I was beginning to think, "Maybe I could do this."

Getting it Over With

After two years of college I had no more money, so I had to go to work for a while and make some money to come back. I was nineteen or twenty. I had a scholarship, but I still had room and board to pay for. So that's why I went to work for the guy who took my virginity.

At that time, four of us were living in a one-bedroom apartment in Des Moines. We were all virgins. (One of us, however, was lying.) None of us had ever seen a condom, which in those days were called "rubbers." (I always thought of them as little raincoats.) Anyway, I took some from Wallace Sundries. We blew one up, put water in it (we were very mature), got bored, and I threw it in my purse along with my lipstick, my wallet and my Sunday Missal (I was still a Catholic). I then proceeded to interview for a job with the guy who took my virginity, and it was quite an interview. While looking for a pen, I pulled out my missal, and lo and behold, the condom was hanging from it. My soon-to-be deflowerer said, "Well, Miss Wallace, that's a hell of a bookmark." It was only a matter of time. And of course I got the job.

I was the only female credit inspector at this credit company. I would call people's neighbors and ask them all about the debtor; it was awful. Even then, before computers, there was no privacy.

I worked there for about six months, and then my grandpa died and left me five thousand dollars, so I went back to school. I stayed in touch with my boss and he kept saying he wanted to be my first, as it were, and I figured, "Oh, well. Maybe it's time. I'm almost twenty-one." So he was on a business trip near my college and we arranged to meet in Burlington, Iowa. At the Voyager Motel. Where I lost my virginity. (But I still didn't *date*, you understand.)

My first sexual experience was hilarious. In books and the movies, you always see the girl crying delicately into the pillow, but I just said, "Ow! Ow!" Well you can imagine how successful that was. "Ow! I hate this! Ow! *Ow!*" My first sexual experience. It went down *very* fast.

I ran into him twenty years later when I was doing a play in Chicago. He was charming. He was in Chicago at a convention, and I said, "Have you told everyone that you took my virginity?" and he said, "Hell, yes—and they don't believe me!"

I was really pretty much a virgin till I was twenty-five. I mean, I had that one less than successful experience in Burlington, but I didn't have my first real relationship until I went to New York, and then who cared what you did? It was great, it was the sixties—you didn't have to worry about anything. That was the time to start having sex.

New York would change everything for me. I left for New York the day I graduated. I'd been looking forward to it all that time. Once I heard that applause, the last year and a half of high school and then college and those two sensational summers, I was ready to go. I was a very big deal, and I was encouraged by the professionals who had come there to teach and work. Nobody gave me their home phone number, but that was fine. I was encouraged. And I was Dodie Goodman's understudy. She still tells people, "You know that girl on *The Bob Newhart Show*? She was my understudy!" Not bad! And on that note, I left for New York.

A Helluva Town

I hope you all remember that most of my New York adventures were told in Chapter One. I lived in that fabulous city for almost a decade, but the neighborhood was starting to change; it became much more upscale and the rents skyrocketed. Needless to say, the landlady was not happy with her hundred and eighty dollars per month rent for my apartment. While I was in L.A., she left a message with my answering service telling me I was evicted. The lovely Doris (that was her name) and her little dog Toto (that was his name) threw my stuff into a box, put it in the basement, and promptly started charging two thousand dollars per month for the apartment. So, ever the optimist, I thought, "Well, this is an opportunity to move to L.A." It was easy. I had no sofa. I had a bowling award from the Broadway Show League, a nice silver-plated trophy with a little bowler on top, a butch-looking lady with a ducktail hairdo. I had a feather boa and some books and records, and that was it.

So L.A. seemed the next logical step. I was on my way.

4 don't look back

→

Sunny
Los Angeles

My first job in L.A. was on a show called *The Storefront Lawyers*, a TV show that had a run of about twenty minutes.

My first West Coast agents, by the way, were Mike Ovitz and Ron Meyer—you know, part of the Creative Artists Agency "triumvirate"—but not for long. I wanted to be submitted for the part of Hot Lips on *M*A*S*H*, even though I admitted it would be way-out casting. They said, "Oh, Marsh—we love you, you know we love you, and we love seeing you come into the office, but this has to be a girl that somebody would actually want to screw." Thanks, guys. I'd hate to think what you'd say to me if you *didn't* love me.

Before I left New York, I was in an off-Broadway production of *Dark of the Moon*. We weren't doing very good business, so the producer/bowling alley entrepreneur said, "Know what we need to do with the lead in this? We need a Playmate of the Year!" *Huh?* The producer/bowling alley entrepreneur got in touch with the then-Playmate of the Year, a woman named Claudia Jennings. Claudia is the only person I ever knew who lied and said she was *older* than she was. (Can you imagine an actress actually doing that? In Hollywood, fourteen-year-old actresses make themselves younger.)

She was very pretty, very kind; I liked her a lot and we became good friends. When I came out to L.A. to do *The Merv Griffin Show*,

I stayed with Claudia and her boyfriend Bobby Hart, who sang with and wrote songs for The Monkees. Then Alison Cannon and I moved into her ex-boyfriend's house, a wonderful house at the top of Laurel Canyon, for a whopping three hundred dollars a month.

Claudia went on to be a B-movie queen, her most notable role being in *Truck Stop Slut*. Before she was thirty, she died in a car crash on The Pacific Coast Highway. An awful shame. I liked her so much. She was a big help at making me feel comfortable about being out here.

My next job was a television pilot called *This Week in Nemtin*. It was kind of a Polish *Laugh-In* starring a pre-*M*A*S*H* McLean Stevenson. It was very, very funny. The guys who did *Nemtin*, Saul Turteltaub and Bernie Orenstein, were great comedy producers, and I loved every minute.

Begin the Benign

It was when I was doing *This Week in Nemtin* that I found the first lump in my breast.

Like a lot of women who developed very early, I have always had the fibroid cystic condition, which in itself is not dangerous; it just makes it difficult to pick up on something potentially dangerous. You have to be really doubly vigilant, and I was very good about it. I had very regular checkups.

I find this big lump, and my ob-gyn says, "I don't think it's any big deal, but you better go see a surgeon." And I'm not scared. Until the surgeon says, "Well, this could be cancer, you know. And here's what we do: we have to stick a needle in it, and if no fluid comes out, then we'll take you to the hospital, put you under, remove the lump, take it to the lab—that's called a frozen section." (This sounded to me like some sort of demented dessert.) "And if it's malignant, we'll come back and we'll take your breast off."

I said, "Hello? Excuse me?"

I had never particularly defied authority, although I'd certainly always had my own opinions, but this was just too barbaric to me. I mean, *really*! Fortunately, they rarely do things that way anymore. They now let a woman wake up and tell her the options and give her a minute to make this decision. But back then, for years and years, that's how women found out they had breast cancer—they woke up all alone in a cold, dark recovery room without a breast. Thinking about those women tears my heart out.

Well, of course I was terrified, but I said, "No!" And he said, "Well, that's how we do it, you know. You have to do it that way."

And I said, "No, I don't."

That's when I got on a plane and went to my hometown, where my Uncle Jimmy was a doctor. He removed the lump, and my sister drove to Des Moines carrying the lump in a Chinese food carton, since they had no lab in Creston, and she sang to the lump all the way: "Begin The Benign"!

The experience was kind of an epiphany for me. I didn't even know what questions to ask. I didn't know anything about options. I didn't know anything about anything. I was just another scared woman listening to a male doctor tell her what to do about her own body. And I thought, "I'm never going to be this scared again, this unprepared. *The doctors can be in charge of my medical treatment, but I am going to be in charge of my health.*"

I vowed to make three changes. First, I'd quit smoking. Second, I'd get off the couch and start some sort of an exercise program. Not my natural bent by a long shot, but we know now the wonderful things exercise does for women—for our bones, hearts, endorphins, and libido. It turns out that regular exercise decreases the risk of getting breast cancer in the first place. And the third area I knew I had to change—big time—was my diet. On that one, I am still a work in progress. Hey, I'm from the Midwest, birthplace of fudge; as far as I'm concerned, chocolate is a vegetable. Well, it *is* a bean.

Not to be outdone in the midst of all this, my dad actually got throat cancer.

We all met him up at the Mayo Clinic. His prognosis was terminal, but he told them, "Tough, but you ain't takin' my voice box. If I can't talk, I don't want to live." And Poke being Poke, they didn't, and he lived.

"Carol" Is Born

I was happy and grateful about my diagnosis, but about to give up on my showbiz career. One day I was out auditioning for a galoshes commercial that was going to run on *Beat the Clock* reruns in Montana somewhere. Driving back, I kept thinking, "This is not a career that's ever going to work out. I should never have done it. It was a big mistake. Who am I kidding?" etc. When I got home, the phone was ringing. It was a woman named Ethel Wynant. She said, "Hello, I'm calling for Grant Tinker; just a moment." Grant Tinker! Handsome-married-to-Mary-Tyler-Moore Grant Tinker! I couldn't believe it. He gets on. "Hello, this is Grant Tinker. We'd like you to be on *The Bob Newhart Show*." Just like that.

Naturally, I thought it was a joke, and I'm amazed that I didn't say anything lewd or rude. I said, "Oh, sure, I'd be happy to come in and read for you."

"No, no, you don't understand," he says. "You have the job."

"Well, I'd be happy to do anything..."

"No, you're wanted. Come in and meet me."

"...clean your office or something..."

No, no, you don't understand, *you have the job*!

What had happened was that the legendary Bill Paley, founder of CBS, had seen me on *The Merv Griffin Show* the night I was so funny. I was auditioning and didn't know it, so I didn't even have to be nervous. Mr. Paley saw the pilot of *The Bob Newhart Show* and wanted to make some casting changes: "Get me that redhead I saw on Merv." Then they wrote in the part of the secretary/receptionist "Carol" just for me.

So I went and met Lorenzo Music for lunch, and he kept saying,

"It's okay, you've got the job. You've got the job." What I couldn't grasp was that when Bill Paley—the boss's boss's boss's boss's boss—hires you, you really do have the job.

Still, I didn't have a clue what I was doing. I was on a network sitcom and kept thinking, "They're going to find me out and they're going to say there's been a terrible mistake." It didn't help that Peter Bonerz, my co-star who played the dentist, watched me rehearse for that first show, made a face like he found me about as funny as a sink full of dirty dishes, rolled his eyes and walked away. (I thought this was terribly rude, so I stopped speaking to him, but of course he didn't notice. Bob had to tell him, "Uh, Pete—Marcia's not speaking to you.")

I had never created a flesh-and-blood character until I created Carol, and I wasn't sure if she, or I, for that matter, could ever win an audience over. But then Carol and I got that great big laugh on the first show, and I thought, "We did it!" The line was, "Well, if I'd known that, I'd have hired a marching band." Hilarious, no? Perhaps you need the context. But it was an astonishing moment, since no one had laughed all week and the night of taping they howled. Hello, show business.

In the years following that opening night of *The Bob Newhart Show*, I have been called "Carol" by fans, friends, relatives and both my parents. (Of course, my father also called me Sherry [my sister], Cecilia [his sister] and Henry [our dog].) Come to think of it, I'll answer to anything.

Just a brief aside about Carol: she was different than most secretaries in a sitcom. She wasn't in love with her boss; she wasn't ditzy or a prim spinster. (In fact, she had a very healthy libido: Carol had romances with Jerry the dentist and Mr. Carlin the neurotic. She even ran off to Dayton, Ohio, with Mr. Borden.) She was a nice person, a hard worker, an optimist and really good at her job. She also had a great sense of humor. In a lot of ways Carol and I were the same person: Midwestern, loyal, funny, optimistic, and we both used our humor as a defense. But—and this is the depressing part—she had a lot more dates. She also met and married the man of her dreams ten years before I did.

In those first six months, I was really, really nervous. Probably because of the way it had happened. I guess I'd often had good luck, but this was *amazing* luck. I had done everything I could do, and when the break came, it was all about being in the right place at the right time.

But... I was not handling it particularly well.

I think what happened was, I kept trying to make the people on the show my family, and they weren't. Also, I didn't know where Carol began and I left off. Or maybe it the other way around.

I'd started to get fan letters, too. Some nice, as if I were Pamela Anderson or somebody. But I got some really weird fan mail, too. One letter, for example, was from a nude guy holding a gun. He was standing under a tree, *au natural,* pointing a gun to the camera, and for reasons known only to himself, he picked me to receive this picture. Fame can get really strange. One night, after I'd started on the Newhart show and come back to New York from L.A. to visit a friend who lived on 8th Avenue, I was walking down the street about ten o'clock or so and I saw this couple going at it in a doorway; they were actually standing there having sex. And the guy—you could just see his face; he looked like Howdy Doody—he lifted up his head, looked at me, and yelled, "Love your work!" I yelled back, "Love yours!" Bob just loves that story.

Woman on the Verge of a Nervous Breakdown

An odd thing was happening: the more successful I became on the show, the worse I felt. I got more and more lonely, more and more isolated; I would go home after the show and feel alone in a way that I never had before.

Around this time I started to have an affair with someone who was a behind the scenes guy on the show. He wasn't married or anything, but he still didn't want anybody to know about us. As you can imagine, that didn't do a whole lot for my self-esteem. Though we liked each other, he wasn't very serious about me, and I'm not sure I was serious about him either. But why was he ashamed to be with me? And why did I accept that?

The affair turned out to be just another way to make me feel isolated and lonely. Everybody on the show was married and had children, and we'd go out to dinner and stuff, and I *still* kept trying to make them *my* family. Suzanne Pleshette, who was always a good friend and always tried to be up front with me, saw how destructive this relationship was for me and said, "Marcia, don't do this. I'm telling you, not just for today, but for your life!"

I started to unravel.

I got through the first year, but after that I began having a real hard time sleeping. And I became bulimic to keep the weight off. I was bulimic before there was a word for it. I heard some star talking openly about her successful method of weight control: "Well, I eat all I want and throw up," she said. Sounded good to me. I'd stopped sleeping in my bed. I'd sleep in my clothes on the couch, or on the floor with the TV on all night. And I really was unraveling.

I had had a headache for about seven years. So I was taking lots of pills—aspirin, Anacin and stuff. Well, one of these had phenobarbital in it—god forbid that I should look at any instructions the pharmacist gave me—and this certainly exacerbated my condition.

Because I didn't deal with the issue of eating, I kept it off by throwing up, by stuffing myself and then fasting. The amount of food I could eat was pretty staggering; my sister says the meals I consumed could feed a small South American country. I guess I felt I wasn't able to lose weight until I got out of my parents' house, because of everything that was going on there. And also—I've thought a great deal about this—if I stayed kind of fat and unpopular, I wouldn't have to make the same choices about getting married that everyone else in high school did. I'd felt like such a victim, but once I gave up my victim papers I realized that being fat was probably my choice as much as not being fat was anybody else's. My weight kept me safe and it ensured that I was going to be able to get out of Creston, Iowa.

The second year of the show started. I came back and Bob said he wanted to talk to me. I realize now how hard this must have been for him. Remember, he only played a shrink. In real life, he is not a guy who likes to talk about personal things. But Bob chose to do this himself and not delegate the job. He is such a decent guy. Anyway, he said, "Marcia, you seem very angry."

I said, *"Really?!"* Because I was totally unaware of it. I guess you don't know, when you're unraveling, that you're unraveling. I wasn't careening off walls, but I cried a lot, I was angry a lot, I didn't sleep, and I was very hyper. Most of my friends' eyes would glaze over and they'd disappear without saying anything, but I remember my friend Joyce telling me, "You're so hyper you're driving me crazy. I just don't even want to be around you!"

And I thought, "I don't know what you're talking about. I'm perfectly calm."

I had a real hate on for the AD, the assistant director, a guy by the name of Greg. A perfectly nice guy, but it seemed to me that he was picking on me. I don't like to be told what to do, you see. I love to be directed, but if it's your job just to tell me what to do arbitrarily, forget it. I wouldn't have done well in the army; I wouldn't do well in prison. I was constantly furious at Greg, and he was only trying to do his job.

Then my birthday came around. I turned thirty-one, and Bob and his wife Ginnie took me out to dinner. I think everybody in the cast was there. I asked my backstage guy if he'd go, and to my shock he said yes. So we went out to dinner, and I said to him, "It's my birthday. Why don't we drive back to your house together?"

And he said, "No, you have to take your own car so you can leave in the morning."

Well, I just lost it, totally, and I started to cry. I cried all the way out there, and I cried all night. Oh, it must have been fun for him—

I cried *all night*; I cried all the next day as I drove back. And when I wasn't crying, I was angry.

My headaches were worse, and I had been taking a lot of Fiorinal, painkillers with phenobarbital. This was the days before those eighty-seven pages of potential side effects they hand out with every prescription. "You got a headache? Here ya go." Well, these pills were major drugs, and hey, if one works, three should be better. After all, I was in the seventh year of this headache. Anyway, they made me more than a little goofy. I didn't drink or anything in those days, but I did take diet pills, and enough so that it surely contributed to the mood swings. You think? Obviously, this was a woman going to pieces.

I started to see it in other people's faces. It began to affect the shows. Only two, but that's more than enough. After one of them, the director said my performance was off, and I tried to joke my way out of it. I made some Richard Nixon joke; I can't remember, "I will not resign" or something stupid like that. Everyone was ha-ha-ing, so I thought from then on everything would be fine.

And then on the following Friday I started to get real dizzy. I went to the doctor and he asked me what I was taking. I told him the diet pills and something for my headache and something for my thyroid.

He said, "That's an awful lot of pills together; that's probably why you're dizzy. Don't worry about it."

People ask me what it's like to totally lose it, to have a complete nervous breakdown. I answer that for me it was like watching a movie of somebody else's breakdown. I remember sitting in a restaurant with my friend Renee Lippin, who played Michelle on the show, sobbing. Not quietly into my napkin, but wracking, heaving sobs, and still I managed to eat two orders of Du-par's pancakes and bacon. I remember trying to ride my bike on the lot during my lunch hour, but I couldn't get it down the steps; I had forgotten how. I was just standing there immobile, holding the handlebars of the bike until somebody from the crew came to help me.

It all came to a head during the filming of an episode, and when I see the show I did that night, I still can't believe it. I answer the phone, and instead of going, "It's for you, Bob," I slam the desk, my eyes like saucers, and scream, *"IT'S FOR YOU, BOB!"* At the end of the show, I felt like I was in a dark tunnel and all these people were outside looking in at me. Actually, everyone *was* looking at me *and* talking about me. Grant Tinker was there, upset and furious with me. Suzanne was very angry with me, Bob was very angry with me. Everybody was.

Finally, it had happened. I had totally unraveled. On national television.

I've always suspected that if it weren't for Ginnie Newhart, that night would have been it for me. But she said, "No, let's try to help her." She insisted that I spend the night at their house, and the next day she called her doctor and he eventually got me into the UCLA Neuropsychiatric Institute, or as I affectionately termed it, The Bin.

The Backstage Guy had been there that night, too. He'd never seen me like that, and he literally cringed from my behavior. I called him up later and he started yelling and screaming at me on the phone, and then he hung up. Hey, I didn't want to deal with me either.

I was awake all night, and I thought, "I'm totally out of control. I've got to do something here. I'm all alone, and if I don't do something, I'm going to lose everything." So the next day I went into Grant Tinker's office and said, "I'm going to check myself into the hospital."

Now, to back up a little, I hadn't ever been in any sort of therapy. But when this whole thing started, I went to a public health place where they gave you new therapists, and they assigned me a lovely guy who thought I was just the most charming thing in the whole world. He couldn't imagine I had a problem: "Why, there's nothing wrong with you!" He was adorable.

But then, of course, seemingly out of the blue, I threw this huge fit, and he seemed shocked, *shocked* at my anger. He'd just hung out his shingle and I had appeared pretty normal. But I was one sick puppy.

Anyway, I said to Grant that morning, "I'm going to check myself into a hospital."

And he said, "You know something, Marcia? We're really glad you're doing this. We like you very much. We don't want you to leave, but this is a business. We're not your family. And if this had continued we would have had to fire you. And we don't want to do that." Which was wonderful, really. At any number of other places I would have been let go earlier. But it was at that very moment that I became the Frances Farmer of sitcom television.

To "The Bin" and Back

I called Dennis Dugan, who was married to my friend Joyce Van Patten at that time, and said, "Will you drive me to The Bin?" And he said, "Sure." He dropped me off with a card that listed twenty-five things not to do in the loony bin: "Don't call the doctors 'Bob,'" "Don't call the nurses 'Suzanne,'" "Chew your food twenty-five times," "Don't f**k your pillow." It was hilarious; I carried it around with me a long time.

He dropped me off, and there I was. Checked myself into the loony bin. Got Judy Garland's old room. And loved it! Absolutely loved it. Well, that's when I figured out that I'd been taking so many of these headache pills that if I had gone off them cold turkey I would have had some sort of seizure and maybe died.

Everyone was so relieved that I was in there, and kind of shocked, too. I think they thought I was just acting out, as opposed to really being in trouble. Suzanne called and said, "MarciaMarcia"— she always called me that, wanting to make sure she got my attention—"I'm so glad you're getting help." And then she and her husband Tommy promptly sent me a fruitcake for Christmas. I love that Suzie.

Bob and Ginnie came to visit me, and she invited all the patients to her house: "Oh, Bob, they're such darling people. Why don't we invite them over?" At one point, Bob was cornered by some true schizophrenic lunatic, who kept saying that he was Jesus, and that what a lot of people didn't know about Jesus was that Jesus was a very good dancer. So here's Bob going, "Uh-huh," like *"Get me out of here,"* and Ginnie's cooing, "Bob, Bob, lets have him over for Thanksgiving." "Uh-huh, uh-huh . . ."

I was in there for three months altogether. It was pretty intense; we had *lots* of group therapy. They kept telling me not to smile so much. "What are you smiling about?" I guess I walked around with a frozen smile on my face, as if there was some sort of award being offered. But I thought, "If I weren't here, I'd be in such big trouble."

So there I was. We had physical therapy and occupational therapy and Crazy Fred. Crazy Fred was the head shrink of the ward. That's where I met him, and he became my shrink for the next seven years. He was great.

After our first three weeks we were allowed to go on the outside. The show had been off for the three weeks I'd been in The Bin, and now it was starting up again. My timing was really good; I slept at The Bin and went to do the show in the daytime. All in all, I only missed one show. Not bad for a dame who went completely loony.

Everybody was really glad to see me back, but mainly it was, "You're *okay* now, Marcia—right?" Listen, in the context of a television show, they shouldn't have had to deal with my craziness. They wouldn't have done me any favors by ignoring my behavior or enabling it; I was actually very lucky that nobody would put up with it. These people liked me and they wanted to help me, but I wasn't their spouse or daughter. I wasn't their responsibility. And I began to understand that. Every single member of that cast—Bob, Suzie, Peter, Bill Daily—everybody wanted only the best for me, but I wasn't their job.

Now, looking back, it's very clear to me what brought it all on. Abusing medication, yes, but that was only part of it. I couldn't deal with being on the show but not being in the family, even a make-believe family. I thought I would feel like I belonged. I expected it to make me happy. I was thin, I was successful, people knew me, and I was getting love letters in the mail. Shouldn't I be fulfilled? Expectations are a bitch.

My best friend Brett Somers always says I went crazy rather than put the weight back on, and it's not that simple, but there's no question that the cushion of a hundred extra pounds can keep those demons at bay. When those hundred pounds went, out came the sadness and rage that I had stuffed inside along with food. And I felt totally, completely vulnerable and unprotected without the weight.

Before the breakdown, I was able to handle things very well for a while. That's why I call it my *Reader's Digest* nervous breakdown, because it was so condensed. I got through the first year of the show fine; nobody knew how isolated I felt. I behaved very well, hid my pain, even though there was a lot of "Marcia, rehearsal's over. You can go now." Still, everything was basically fine. And I was very grateful and very funny and a very good girl.

Then in the summer between the first and second years of the show, I started having that affair with the backstage guy. But he didn't want anyone to know about it, so I had nobody saying "I'm with her." It's not even that I was in love with him. But just his refusal to acknowledge me brought up all kinds of painful memories and played into my low self-esteem. There I was, thin and successful and having an affair, and *still* lonely and unhappy, full of self-loathing, and hearing my mother's voice: "You're fat and ugly and no one will ever love you."

It seemed for years and years and years, I picked men who were like my mother: somebody who was going to be very critical and not available. I mean, I didn't pick my father. I went for emotional abuse, not physical—relationships that would let me go home and think, "I'm nothing, I'm nobody, and my mother's right."

But an awful lot of anger started to come out, too, and that scared me. Because clearly the weight had kept the anger in for a long time. That's why whenever I see my son Mikey throw huge fits, I'm jealous! I'd have loved to have done that. Tantrums—I wanted to throw a couple of tantrums. But nobody's interested in an adult tantrum; they're no fun to be around.

I wasn't sure I wanted to leave The Bin. I was happy as a clam there; somebody had to feed me, I had a place to sleep, I could throw a fit there if I wanted to, and I even had some sort of makeshift family. But finally it was time to go, and I left.

One night shortly after I was released from The Bin, I had a terrible, terrible anxiety attack, and I raced to UCLA and tried to get back in. They said, "Well, we'll let you back in, but you have to stay on another floor." Not good! I had gone to see a movie called *Don't Look Now*. You remember that? With the little red dwarf? It was the scariest, most unnerving movie, and it terrified me so that it sent me, in the middle of the night, to try to get back into The Bin again.

To this day I don't know what scared me so much about that movie. It was very primal, about dead children—it was sexual, it was brutal. It reminded me of a recurring dream I had when I was a little kid. I was in charge of a swimming pool, but every time I would stop a baby from falling in, another baby would fall in, and all you could see was dead babies in the bottom of the swimming pool. Guess who those were? I must have perceived myself on some level to be in danger, and I think in many ways I was. Part of it was never being allowed to express anything of my own darker nature, and I have plenty. That's one of the things I love about Mikey; he has such a lightness about him. Maybe because he says what's on his mind.

Crazy Fred, the Shrink

Now, I wasn't home free yet, but I was not in any trouble with the Newhart show. I finished with the hospital. I was much better, but I was still very shaky. And I went into therapy with Dr. Frederick Silvers. I called him Crazy Fred, no doubt to get a rise out of him. "You know I call you Crazy Fred." He said, "I'd prefer if you called me

Crazy Frederick. My name is Frederick." Dr. Silvers was a Jungian therapist, and he dealt with dreams. He was a great shrink, but, as many the shrink, he had his wacky side. (I sent him to my dentist once, and my dentist called me and said, "Whatever he owes me, he can forget about. I just don't ever want to see him again. I can't stand it. He drove me to Valium. I'm on Valium, Marcia!") Shrinks *are* a little loony.

Looking back, I realize that his office was the safest place I've ever been, because when I was with him I went absolutely crazy. Talk about transference: I made him my mother, my father—I even made him the Dairy Queen guy. I made his life a living hell. He told me once that my time was up, and I refused to leave. He got up and I grabbed him by the leg. He was trying to leave the room: "Come on, Marcia. Time's up. Come on.

"No, I'm not leaving." I wanted to have temper tantrums, and I did, one right after another. I hated every minute of it, and it's a testament to my tenacity and perverse kind of guts, really, that I stayed. And continued to confront my demons.

I think this is an interesting story (you'll be the judge of that): Frederick dealt a lot with the *animus*. And in my dreams, the animus was an incubus. Had a big penis and a tail. And he followed me wherever I went. I couldn't get away. I would slam the door in his face; he would come in and burn the house down. I'd try to get him out; he'd blow up the house. I'd hide in the closet; he'd come in with a knife. These dreams went on for years and years and years. Then he stopped looking like an incubus. He started looking like an FBI guy. One of those guys with crew cuts? And still he would follow me and follow me. I'd just make it into the house. But then he'd set the house on fire. I'd just make it into the car, and then the car would blow up. He'd stalk me with guns or knives. Horrible stuff.

And then one day, after years and years and years, I turned to him in a dream and said, "What do you want?"

And he said, "I just want to talk to you."

When I told Frederick, he said, "You did it. We did it!" I integrated. I turned around and said, "You're part of me, and I'm having no luck trying to get you."

It was amazing. Dr. Silvers started celebrating, and he said, "You are brave; you just never gave up." He gave me all the credit.

Now during this whole time I'd accused him of being *everything*. No wonder those shrinks kill themselves, with people like me. And he never gave up. I'd say, "You know, I think I'm psychotic; I'm starting to hallucinate." And he'd say, "You're not." He'd always bring me back. It must have been exhausting. "You're fine. You're here. You're going to do this. You can do this." He's a real bodhisattva. Most people aren't willing to work that hard. But I had to get rid of this darkness. And then that was it. He said, "You're done." And basically, I was.

Three's a Crowd

But there was still stuff.

Backing up a little, after I got out of The Bin, I'd go from time to time to visit my friend Kent in New York. We were in The Fourth Wall group together back in the sixties. He directed me in *Dark of the Moon*. We were very close friends who had stayed in touch even after I moved to L.A. His friend, a very handsome guy named Gene about six years younger than me, decided suddenly that he wanted to have a relationship with a woman. Namely me.

And I, of course, was *unbelievably* vulnerable. So we had this affair. It was a joke; you could barely call it sex. (Hello, earth to Marcia: he's *gay*.) But I was so needy I didn't care. And he was *so* eager. I guess I should never have told him I had Judy Garland's old room at The Bin. Of course, it became a triangle. I've had a lot of triangles in my life. I suppose they started with my mom and dad; my mom telling my dad to beat me up, my dad telling me *way* too much information about their sex life, my mom saying "Your father hates you," my father saying "Your mother hates you," and me trying to please them both.

I think a lot of women get into triangles; I don't think I'm so unusual in that.

So, there we were, me and Gene and Kent. And all Gene wanted to do was come to California and become a star. He was really handsome. I introduced him to as many people as I could. I remember one producer saying to me, "Marcia, forgive me, but isn't this boyfriend of yours gay?" I don't remember what I said—something like, "Well, I don't know, but we're together..." I embarrassed myself terribly. But it was something I needed to do.

When I told Brett everything, when I said, "Brett, I need to do this," she was so wonderful. She just said, "Okay. Okay, hon, whatever you say."

I guess I should digress for a minute here and talk about Brett, because she was there through all of this.

I met Brett Somers on *The Match Game*, which I started doing when I'd just gotten out of The Bin. Brett had one of the few dressing rooms, and she was willing to share with other women on the show. The first thing she said to me was, "You'll have to forgive me because I'm not myself; I just separated from my husband." (That was Jack Klugman). And I said, "I didn't notice anything was wrong; I just got out of The Bin." And we were best friends from that day forward. Even though she *loves* to boss me around. We've been through a lot together; we've shared so many things. She directed me in a play, we bought an apartment together, we went to the same hairdresser. When it came time to get married, I said, "You know, I have a sister; she'll be the maid of honor," and she said, "To hell with her! I'm your maid of honor!" We were so close people thought we were lesbians! When we stayed up in Carpenteria in the little condominium we bought together, our neighbors winked at us and said, "You know, if you girls ever have a fight, we have a spare bedroom."

I looked at Brett and said, "My social life isn't bad enough, now they think I'm a dyke!"

She, of course, got ever so coquettish and talked about her children and her ex-husband, and all I had was a niece!

Brett can be awful bossy. But on the important things she never judges you. Still, she always lets you know what's on her mind. I sent her a thing from a birthday book, and her birthdate said "The day of the unsolicited opinion." Just like the Wallaces, everybody's entitled to her opinion, too.

Anyway, I'm having this ridiculous affair with this ridiculous guy who everybody knows is gay. Everybody else thinks I'm in a lesbian affair with Brett Somers. Hell, even *I* know he's gay, but I just needed somebody to be nice to me. Remember the end of *Some Like It Hot* when Jack Lemmon confesses to his suitor Joe E. Brown that he's really a man? "Well, nobody's perfect," was the answer, and boy, did I identify with that. But then something ugly happened. We had a huge fight—over what, I can't remember—and he moved out. I felt relieved.

He went back to New York, and then, of course, I began to miss him. (Remember, nobody's perfect.) I kept calling him, but he never answered me. So I flew to New York. I went down to his apartment and found him in bed with a guy. You see scenes like this in the movies all the time. People scream or cry or shoot people. I did none of those. I just felt unbelievably hollow and lonely.

I went back to my hotel and called Kent. When I told him what happened, he started yelling at me, "You've made a fool of yourself, and you're trying to make this more than it is," and he hung up on me.

I heard this horrible, horrible sound—animal, primal, guttural—it was me, screaming. I had a glass in my hand. I slammed it down; it broke. I was holding a shard of glass. I started shoving it into my stomach. And this voice in me said, "You'd better be very sure before you do that. You're all alone in a hotel in New York City, and there's nobody here who loves you anymore. Be very sure you want to do this." And I didn't. I put it down. And I'm not saying that by the next day I was fine, but I started to reverse the trend. I was thirty-two by then. And I'm very grateful I didn't kill myself.

When I was twenty, I went to a psychic who warned me that somewhere down the line I would have a breakdown and become suicidal. Well, I thought that was about the silliest thing I'd ever heard. Me? Resident good sport and jolly fat girl? A breakdown? Hah! I threw my head back and *laaughed*! Well, kids, never say never, because it'll come right back and bite you in the ass.

Each day I got stronger, each day I felt more myself, each day I became more okay.

I ran into Gene on the street years later. He was so glad to see me, and I was just so embarrassed. But when I look back—well, who of us doesn't have liaisons that we are *highly* embarrassed by, or would never do again?

I can't say that after that whole thing I immediately began to choose the right men; I didn't. But I had hit bottom. I began choosing a little bit better and I didn't feel as bad. As I said, the trend was reversing itself.

I guess my breakdown wasn't so *Reader's Digest*-y after all. It lasted about two years. And eventually I was able to let the job be just the job.

And let the bad affairs go. But I put up a fight. I was always saying to Fred, "Boy, Gene'll never get over me, will he?" And Fred would say, "He couldn't wait to get away from you, believe me."

Meanwhile, Back in Iowa

Meanwhile, while all of this was going on with me, my family back in Iowa were amazed that I'd gotten on a hit TV show. My parents decided that they were real wrong about me. My sister said they switched alliances immediately from her to me. I don't think it was that simple. But nobody ever expected much of me, so when it happened, they were astonished and thrilled. I told you my dad used to sell my old gym socks; he sold everything I gave him. Johnny Carson gave me an autographed picture for him, and wrote on it, "To Poke—

don't sell this." My father would corner everybody he met: "Say, have you seen that Bob Newhart show?" And if they'd say no, he'd say, "Just wondering." But if they said yes, he'd say, "That's my daughter!" So it gave both my parents a new lease on life. It made them stars.

And I resented that a little.

I guess I was expecting a big change from them. In any case, I was through being the good little girl. So I started trying to talk to them about the past.

The first time I tried to talk to my father, he said, "I know, your mother hated you. I told you that before." That was his answer to everything. What about all those beatings? Oh, well, yes, "but it was for your own good." *It was for your own good!*

My relationship with my sister has been very loaded, too, because we are so different, but she is the one person I can always count on. Anyway, my parents were both very happy to see me on TV, and they both felt, "Oh, hey—we were kind of wrong about her."

Then (talk about you can't go home again) in 1965—it was before the Newhart show, but I was on *The Merv Griffin Show*—my hometown asked me to come back. The town was 150 years old and they asked me to come back and be part of the sesquicentennial celebration.

I'd had a teacher I adored by the name of Dave Rissler, who was the music teacher. I always thought he should have been a performer. He was terribly funny. Anyway, he and I were going to do these improvs together.

Well, please. They changed the location from the auditorium to the football field. So there we were on this stage the size of a postage stamp doing these improvs. And every night the California Zephyr would come by in back and everything would start to shake, and the entire audience would turn and look at the train going by. I swear to god, we followed a cow act; her name was Cookie. She drank strawberry pop and prayed. They had trained her to put her little hooves together. She'd put her head heavenward and go, "Moooooo!"

And then the announcer: "N-o-o-w-w we h-a-a-v-e Cre-s-s-ton's o-o-own"—and the guy didn't know me; he kept mispronouncing my name—"Ma-a-a-a-a-rtha Wa-a-a-a-a-ler!" It was a nightmare. And somehow the gossips in the town decided I was making a bundle. "Did you hear how much she's getting paid? And she's not even any good!" I bombed so bad. Talk about the wrong venue for a touch of light comedy. The two of us out there on the football field, on that tiny stage again and again and again. And we were miked up to this awful public address system. One night I couldn't take it, and I blurted your basic obscenity, and over the P.A. system you heard, "Fu-c-c-k-k-k-k!" Well, that got them back from the California Zephyr real quick. And my dad said, "You can never please them; you can never please them." You really can't go home again, especially with a lousy P.A. system.

Comedy Divine

The Bob Newhart Show was part of the Saturday night lineup that became part of the culture of the seventies. Now, a network is thrilled with 17 million people, but on a given Saturday night, 35 million people or more would be watching those shows. *All in the Family*, *M*A*S*H*, *The Mary Tyler Moore Show*, *The Bob Newhart Show*, and *The Carol Burnett Show*. And (talk about your Dark Ages) a whole family would be watching in front of *one* television set. This was before cable, where you now have seven hundred channels and still can't find anything you want to watch, and before people could afford more than one TV.

Anyway, our show reran in the eighties, went on Nick at Night in the nineties, and is currently on TV Land. It was a dream job playing a swell character, and I wish it for every actor. Being in the big time on the show did finally give me a sense of myself and further possibilities of what I wanted to do. I had agents working for me, but because of the breakdown I was never able to capitalize on that. If I hadn't had that nervous breakdown, I might have been able to parlay the Mike Ovitz connection into something. But I was just grateful that I didn't get fired and couldn't really ask for more money.

Moneywise, I've never made it to the big time in television. I started out on the Newhart show being paid scale, and ended up making twenty-two hundred dollars a show, pretty paltry by *Friends* standards but a fortune when I compare it with what my father used to make.

The breakdown did hold me back, and that's why I was so anxious to get on another series. You know that great apocryphal story that was attributed to Edmund Gwenn? George Cukor said to him, "Oh, dear friend, I'm so sorry you're dying; it must be very hard." And Gwenn said, "Yes, but not as hard as doing comedy." I've heard that from a lot of people, but I'm so happy doing comedy. I've never been somebody who wanted to do *draaaama*. Or even movies, which is fine, since there hasn't been a groundswell movement for my movie career.

I love doing sitcoms; it's the best job in the world for an actor. And those people who quit are just fools. Fools! Because it's like doing a play, only it's great hours. Great money. You get rehearsal. And then you only work twenty-two weeks a year. So then you can do theater, which I've done for years and years. I go on the road a lot. As far as my ambition goes, I'd love to have my own show, yes. And I want to do theater and I want to do sitcoms. Fine by me.

5 don't look back

Bad Sex in the City

Spring, 1977
Omaha Dinner Theater

Dearest Brett,

Remember how encouraged I've been since I stopped meeting only gay guys at every turn? Well, here we go again in, of all places, Omaha, Nebraska. I'm here doing dinner theater and they seem to be everywhere. The producers, the director, the co-star, the waiters, my dentist... I think I even met a gay dog. I have an actual date on Monday with a straight guy, but he is possibly the shortest person on the planet. But cute, and if I can find him, I'm sure we'll have a swell time.

The producers are lovers; one of them has the attention span of a gnat and the other is a genuine manic-depressive. One day he's scrubbing the walls of my dressing room, and the next he'll hide my costume. Basically, they are pleased as punch since we are doing the best business in the history of the theater. And after we close here we go to the Pheasant Run Theater in Chicago. I mean, they're expecting us, we were invited, we're not just showing up with our props in hand.

I enclose excerpts from the reviews. I'm not sending the complete reviews because in dinner theater they don't like to leave anybody out. I got very good reviews, but so did the macaroni salad and the chairs, which does dilute the theatrical impact somewhat. I say, let the chairs

63

*send out their own reviews. I was relieved to see they do remove all
sharp instruments before the show begins, lest a disgruntled theatergoer
gets any ideas.*

Love,
Marcia

After my nervous breakdown, after I was back on the show, I started going on the road every year and doing plays. I went back to Omaha to do *Last of the Red Hot Lovers*, and that's where I met John.

Mr. Close

John was a guy I went to high school with. His father delivered me. (He was a doctor; he didn't just bring me to the house.) And we had quite a nice romance, John and I. (In Omaha, I mean, not in high school.) But of course with my need to beat life into something and to overextend it, I couldn't just leave it at that. After the play was over, I had to say, "Oh, come out to California and move in with me." So he bought a Jeep—he was an eye guy by now, an optician; he did contact lenses—and he came out to L.A and we lived together for a couple of years, which was about one year too long.

I was thirty-five by then and this was really my first relationship where we went places as a couple; I was a very late bloomer in this area. But if it wasn't football or Jeeps, he wasn't too interested. And like a lot of the guys in my life back then, his job was to point out my flaws. I remember him saying once, "I don't know why I like you, since you're not pretty and you don't have a good body."

I thought, "Jeez, there's got to be a better way of phrasing that!" But I didn't realize at the time that I was picking another man who was like my mother: critical and not all that crazy about me.

Anyway, if he wasn't pointing out my flaws, he was puttering around with his Jeep or watching football games. So it's not like I was having such a good time, either. But I was going to make it work; I was going to *make* it work.

And I thought if I had a baby—oh, ho, ho—so we tried. Thank god it didn't work, because that would have been a disaster. It began to be really bad for us after our first Thanksgiving together. We had a huge fight over who would make the stuffing; he had his recipe and I had mine. He had sixteen loaves of bread drying out in the back yard, and I had sixteen drying out inside. Anyway, we didn't speak for weeks. That wasn't a good sign.

Then he started staying out all night with Ed. Ed's-for-Tile, my sister's third husband. They picked up girls together. How sweet.

I want to digress again for a second here and talk about my sister. I was jealous of her back then, because "Mom always liked her best." And she was so cute and so popular. And she, *she* says she was jealous of me because I was so full of life. Go know! What I do know is that I love her dearly, that I couldn't imagine my life without her, and that we are totally committed to this relationship, this incredible sisterhood.

Well, as I said, when all this happened with John, Sherry was on her third husband. Her first husband was a guy named Wallace. She had two babies in the first year of that marriage. Sometimes he abused her; hey, it's what she knew. Once it was so bad he took her to a doctor who said to her, in 1964 in the U.S.A., he said, "What did you do to make him so mad?" And then he said, "You're fine. Go home and be better to your husband." This is one of the most chilling stories I've ever heard in my life.

Alcohol abuse sucks the life right out of a family. People do and say things they regret terribly, but because these words and actions have landed, you can't take them back. Terrible things were done in our house when Sherry and I were growing up, almost all of them alcohol-related. Oh, sure, it was the fifties, and everybody drank in the fifties. But in some families, booze meant trouble; who knows why? Maybe my father was right. From the time we were kids, he used to meet us at the door and smell our breath. We'd say, "Dad, we're eight." He'd say, "Never mind; it's in the blood." Anyway, Sherry and her ex-husband have both been clean and sober for years, and like everybody alive today, wish they had made different choices. But, hey, (close book, look at cover) don't look back, we're not going that way.

Like a lot of girls in the fifties, Sherry had wanted to get away from home, and the way to do it back then was to get married. (Crazy me, I went to New York, waved off by friends who acted as if I was on my way to some TB sanitarium. "No husband? Poor baby." A few years later these same friends would ask, "Still not married? Oh, well, there's time." And years after that, it was: "Tell her never to get married.") Anyway, Sherry got engaged to her first husband while she was still in high school. She was so young; she had *no* idea. Her only hesitation in getting married was that he had the same last name and she wouldn't be able to change hers. *So* young.

My parents were dead set against it. My father was a man with a mission: Stop This Wedding. He cajoled, he threatened, he bullied. One day he was sitting in the store with Aunt Cecilia, and he shot to his feet. "Wait a minute—they've got the same last name; maybe they're related, and that's against the law!" And he tore off to the courthouse, only to be confounded one more time. Finally, Sherry wore him down and they got married. I was, of course, her maid of honor, and looked about forty-five in my lovely pink dress and dyed-to-match pumps. (I never quite figured out why, but there was a time when strangers off the street came up and asked me to be in their wedding. I ended up with about twelve truly terrifying bridesmaid dresses and matching pumps. Not that many friends, but *reeeeeal* popular as a bridesmaid.)

Sherry's son Randy was born, and just over a month later, she got pregnant again with her daughter Kimberly, who was born prematurely.

Kim was born with cerebral palsy, and they told Sherry she wouldn't live till morning. They just came in and said, "Hon, your baby'll be dead before morning." I mean, unbelievable! And then they had to come back and say, "Oh, well ... she's not." And for all the prenatal stuff and how they keep babies alive, Kim did it the old-fashioned way; she screamed for six weeks and strengthened her lungs, and was meant to be here. She weighed two pounds when she was born. She's such a survivor, and one of my favorite people in the world.

Sherry's second husband was a bigamist, and boring. A boring bigamist with bad breath. An alliterative thing. It's worse to be boring than a bigamist. Sherry found out the hard way. Kim just hated him. And finally he said one day, when Kim was about eight, "I'm leaving." And Kim said, "Let me help you pack." And so he left.

Sherry and the kids followed me to California, and then my sister put in her very difficult years drinking. I was a great enabler; I gave her tons of money and tried to take care of her kids and everything. But all that's over now; she's been clean and sober for twenty-one years, a considerable achievement.

And then she met Ed. Ed's-For-Tile. And Ed's-For-Tile and John were very close friends; they used to do some serious drinking together. Then they took to staying out all night and coming back with these stories about how they'd just had to pull over and close their eyes for a minute. Please! They were screwing the world! Just hilarious.

I did learn to scuba dive with John, which is something I enjoyed very much. As a matter of fact, he stayed out all night the night before I was supposed to take my test to get my scuba-diving license. Besides not having had any sleep the night before, I won the Golden Drama-mine Award that day, because all I did was throw up. I was very popular on board the boat.

By this time John was getting letters from old girlfriends. But that thing in me, that tenacity which has worked so well for me most of my life, has sometimes been destructive, because I wouldn't let go. I wouldn't. I'm much better about it now. But then... Anyway, John started having an affair with a friend of my friend Claudia's. Finally, finally I had to admit that this was not working. So that John moved out, and I went on the road with a different John.

Mr. Closer

Now this new John was *soo* talented and smart and funny and sexy, and he drank. A lot. I had been asked to do *Same Time Next Year* at the Traverse City Playhouse in Michigan. I got to pick the guy, and had seen John in a bank commercial. I looked him up in the Players Directory and the rest, as they say, is history.

But, please—you're on the road playing lovers, you don't have to cook, you barely have to do laundry, you're in a hotel. What's not great about it? The perfect climate to fall in love. And I thought I broke the mold with him, because he didn't find any flaws in me; he didn't see anything to criticize—at least not until real life came in. But certainly not in the throes of the affair.

As I said, we got to play lovers on stage. Unfortunately, all of the sexual tension went into our lives, so I wasn't so good on the stage. I was sort of bland; I just sort of stood there. I got one of the worst reviews of my life: "This is the eleventh time I've seen this play, and it's the best production I've ever seen, but I hate Marcia Wallace. It's a two-character play, and he blows her off stage!" And that was it; he did. I just handed it over to him, because I was so happy to be having this wonderful love affair where the guy thought I was fabulous.

As Brett says, "There's only two things to do on the road: have sex or shop," and I've never been much of a shopper. I adored him, and he adored me. We had great conversations, and we stayed up all night, and did all the things you do when you're having a great love affair. But it's not real life. There're no bills and no kids and no laundry, and in the end John and I didn't make that transition into real life. As my beloved friend Peter Allen wrote, "Love Is Easy On The Weekends." You've got to be able to face each other in the bright glare of Monday morning and still find life together exciting.

A Big Impact ... On Myself

In those days, I would always fall; I always had accidents. I had vowed that no one would ever hit me again, but I did a pretty good job on myself. I mean, every time I turned around, I'd trip, or I'd dive head-first into a car and get a concussion, or I'd fall downstairs. Every year around the time of my birthday I was always hurting myself. Always. One time I was going for a job and I leaned over the dishwasher and stabbed myself in the mouth. Honest to god. What are the chances of that? Your hands are busy, so you stab yourself "no hands." This isn't easy! And then later I would accidentally hurt Mikey—slam his fingers in the door. It's amazing that the child welfare department wasn't camped on my doorstep. This was before I was a Buddhist, though; when I started to really commit to Eastern religion, I began to respect myself. But before then? People go through their whole lives and never take the falls I've taken.

But that was my way of dealing with my pain. Because I'd made the vow that no one would ever hit me again around the time of my breakdown, I used to hit myself. I don't know; I've met some people who pull their hair out. It's a variation on the same theme. Sometimes I'd get so mad I'd just have to whack myself. I don't do any of this stuff anymore, though, so when horrible things started to happen in the nineties, really horrible, like death and fire and destruction, I had run out of things. Anything I picked to do, like break down or try to kill myself, I'd done already. And I hate to be redundant.

Anyway, I decided, "All right, I've got to get it together now." I hadn't met Mr. Close, let alone Mr. Right. And I'd had about three dates in my thirties other than the two Johns. First I had the blind date with the cop who broke his foot kicking in a door that was open.

And then I had a relationship with an actor. A mutual friend introduced us, and I became his nighttime girlfriend, which was unfortunately my m.o. in my twenties and thirties; I sold myself short big-time. This guy would phone at seven o'clock, eight o'clock, nine o'clock at night and say, "Can you come over?" He was on a lot of TV shows, and I used to get to sit there and watch him circle the shows he'd been on in the *TV Guide*. Every rerun. He would circle them, set his alarm, and get up and watch himself. Every time he was on TV.

Well, he was tired a lot, and crabby. Thank goodness VCRs came along; I'm sure it made his life a lot easier. And I found out later that one of my dear friends had actually been his daytime girlfriend.

Anyway, I knew he was in therapy—like, all the time. This particular day he calls and says, "Do you want to go out to dinner at some friends' house?" I should have been suspicious. But I said, "Oh, yes, oh, yes, oh, yes." Well, it turns out to be his shrink's house. Now, there he is, Mr. TV Actor, who is this shrink's patient, and there's another girl who's also his patient. And I'm thinking, "Oh, I guess this is fine," and he has this big den with these big beds all over, and TVs on, and everybody's *very* friendly, and finally I think, "Hmm, there's something, hmm..."

Well, evidently Mr. TV had told his shrink that I was good in bed, and so the shrink said, "Let's have some group sex here." Mr. TV didn't ask me. I might have said yes; it wasn't something that I had done or thought much of, but I'd been pretty open to all possibilities, and it was, after all, the seventies. But he didn't *ask* me. I was really angry when it was clear to me what was going on. So I did what I usually do in this situation; I went down to the kitchen and I ate everything I could find. I ate an entire loaf of bread. I ate and ate and ate, and it couldn't fill the hole. That's how angry I was, and that's how empty I felt. I thought, "Something's got to change in the way I view myself and my own worth. Sex is certainly not the way."

So that was it for me and Mr. TV. And here's the sad part—this had been one of my more successful relationships.

And on it went. I had a blind date with another guy one time. He didn't have a couch; he just had a saddle in the middle of his room. To make conversation, I said, "What do you do?" And he said, "Well, I killed a guy once." This was how we started the conversation. When I left that night, I ate an entire dozen donuts.

6 don't look back

Bad Sex in the City, Part 2: Looking for Mr. Close

Christmas 1982

Hi Wendy,

Well, Christmas is coming (I've always been right on top of things) and I hope you're feeling great. I myself have had a wonderful year. I produced a play, started singing, hosted a talk show, turned forty, and met Mr. Right (or at the very least, he's Mr. Close.) It has indeed been a year of nervous breakthroughs.

A year ago, I got tired of sitting around hoping The Love Boat *would call, and I gave myself a job. My manager Judy Thomas and I produced a play called* An Almost Perfect Person, *and my best friend Brett Somers (Suzanne's niece) directed. (A perfect choice on my part, I felt, as she had been telling people what to do for years).*

Michael Bell and Bob Sampson were also in the play. Michael was the first person I met when I came to L.A.; it was when we were hired as stand-ins for the pilot of a celebrity game show. I worried that Michael and Brett would not get along, but they loved each other and he proceeded to refer to her as Madam Lubitsch. So much for my amazing intuition.

We didn't know who to cast as the romantic leading man; I had a huge fight over this with my friend Charlie when I said, "I've never had a romance on stage before, and I'm a little nervous. If I had my druthers, I'd just as soon the guy be straight." He fires back, "Oh, sure, I suppose you'd just say to Laurence Olivier, 'Sorry, Larry, you can't do the part because you're bisexual.'" (I don't really believe in bisexuality except for the English; must be all those boarding schools.)

And here's another example of life's little comeuppances: there I was worrying about the sexuality of the guy I was casting, and we found out later that several guys who came to audition thought Judy, Brett and I were lesbians. Oh, dear—so many lessons, so little time. Anyway, we cast Bob Sampson and opened to very nice reviews (a rare treat for me; my last review said, "She was so bad she ruined other people's performances—she should go back to game shows.") And we ran for sixteen weeks. It was a fabulous experience—for the first time as an actor, I didn't have to hear about how I was too tall, too short, too fat, too thin or too old, because the producer loved me.

Well, honey, we hit the big four-oh this year, me on November 1st (All Saints' Day, dontcha know) Did you mind? I say, "Fine by me." Oh, sure, sure, one day I drove to the post office, walked to the mailbox, and mailed my keys. And sure, sure, one morning I took out the trash, threw away my purse and drove off with the garbage in the seat next to me. But I doubt that these incidents had a thing to do with my turning fuh... fuh...

Word may not yet have hit your block that I am currently singing up a storm, now that I study with the fabulous David Craig, but it's only a matter of time. In spite of an occasional setback, like my obscene phone caller. This guy had been calling for weeks, and I tried everything: blowing a whistle in the phone, talking mean, talking dirty... and then one night I broke into two choruses of "People Will Say We're in Love," and he never called back. Everybody's a critic.

I've also been hosting a talk show (along with Gordon Jump) on the Cable Health Network called Do or Diet. *What's the Cable Health Network, you ask? I believe it's on twenty-four hours a day in Guam. I*

had a great time, though. There I was, ex-chubbette, Queen of the
Twinkies, talking health and nutrition with the biggies. It was creative
casting on the producer's part and I was thrilled to be chosen.

There's also life's little levelers in show business, too. After appear-
ing on approximately a thousand game shows, I had to go in this morn-
ing to audition for a new one. I thought, "Well, it's probably a real hard
game, and they want to make sure I can handle it." It was bingo.

As regards the possible Mr. Right, he's a lawyer and his name is
Marvin. Stay tuned . . . but right now, I can't get this smile off my face.
Food falls out of the corners of my mouth. (Wildly attractive, as
always.)

I hope you're feeling strong and happy and I hope you have a
wonderful year, dear friend. Love to all.

> *Love,*
> *Marcia*

Now I was into the eighties and Ben. Ben was a blind date—literally, a blind guy. Who *also* pointed out my flaws. When he was
giving me a massage one night and complaining about my body, I
said, "*You're blind!* What do you mean 'cellulite'? You're not supposed
to be able to see!" And we're not talking about Tom Cruise here; this
guy was funny-looking, that's the thing. I'd pick all these geeky-look-
ing guys who couldn't find enough fault with the way I looked. I actually pointed this out to Ben once when he just wouldn't let up about
the way I looked: "I hate your hair, I hate your clothes, I hate your
body—"

I said, "Excuse me, are you Paul Newman? I mean—oh, yes,
well, you're right. But you're blind!"

Ben was also a sex therapist. He had written a book on getting
over a broken heart. And he believed in lots of swinging; group sex
and stuff.

After about six months, he takes me on a trip to Puerto Vallarta and almost immediately announces, "This isn't working; you make me nervous." He couldn't tell me that in L.A.? He couldn't tell me that I made him nervous in L.A.? He had to bring me to Mexico to dump me?

I Zigged When I Should Have Zagged

Of course, the definitive story for that is Ziggy. I had an affair with a guy named Ziggy, and we went to Jamaica together. So there we are in Jamaica and it's very romantic and everything, and he turns to me and says, "Do you find the more you like someone the less you want to have sex with them?" I say, "Mmm . . . no." And he says, "Well, I do." So there I am in a Jamaican paradise with a guy who's telling me, "I like you so much I don't want to come near you."

After the debacle with Ben, I started to think once again, "All right, I'm a late bloomer and a slow learner, but somehow I've got to change this. I've got to make myself more available, open up." Brett, of course, had an answer: "Well, hon," she said, "you don't know how to flirt. You've either got it or you don't, and you don't. I've got to teach you to flirt."

I was a disaster. I didn't know how to flirt, I didn't know how to date. I never had a date in high school. I had my first affair when I was twenty-five, my first sexual experience at twenty-one. I had a boyfriend in college but there wasn't much going on between us. It turned out he didn't know it, I didn't know it, but it turned out that he was gay.

So, I said to myself, "You just have to open up your heart and you have to be available. You're an interesting woman; you have things going for you." I kept telling myself that. "You're an interesting woman. You're an interesting woman." So I thought, "No more fix-ups; I'm going to go out with anyone who asks. I'm going to date."

Now, I met this guy on an airplane. I was on my way to do a play in Texas at the St. Edwards Theater. *Light Up The Sky* was the play, one of those plays that goes on longer than bad sex.

The day I met the director, he gripped my shoulders with major liquor on his breath and said, "My mother just died. I want you to wear her furs." I said, "Uhh … okay." Then he wanted to show me where she died, and I swear to god there was a dent in the bed just like Norman Bates's mother. And then he tried to stick his tongue in my mouth. What a guy. My husband was played by a nineteen-year-old student who tried to age by putting lots of white powder in his hair, which kept making us all sneeze on stage. We sneezed our heads off and he still looked only nineteen with powder in his hair.

I played Frances, and the character of my mother, Stella, was played by a darling woman who was a little long in the tooth.

She kept calling me Stanley. (Stanley, Stella—I think she was frozen in a production of *A Streetcar Named Desire*.) Anyway, we played in the round, and occasionally she made her entrance calling out to me, "Stanley, Stanley…" Sometimes she just kept walking and went back to her dressing room. Leaving me there in the dead woman's furs. No wonder I was willing to fly to Dallas for a date with a total stranger.

Marcia Does Dallas

So on my day off, I accepted the invitation from the guy on the plane to come to his house in Dallas. I flew out there, and when I arrived at his house he told me he had to step out for a few minutes. Well, he left me there for *twelve hours*. There was nothing to do, nothing to eat. I looked in his refrigerator and all I found was soy powder and cocaine. I love these types who won't touch sugar ("Oh, my, no, it's *bad* for you") but think nothing of a little heroin. Your basic health nut/drug addict.

Eventually one of his friends shows up and explains that his friend is trying to get over his obsession with a younger woman. Isn't that terrific? The guy finally comes back, apologizes, and says, "I'm sorry I spoiled your good time. I'll be right back." Then he disappears again. Finally I take a cab back to the airport. All the way around, a fabulous date.

Stick Out Your Sandwich and Say "Ahhhh"

Speaking about the director's dead mother reminds me of John Number One's mother. She hated me. All mothers hated me. My own mother, too, although we made up. But what is it with mothers? My friend Natalie's mother liked me. But boyfriends' mothers? John's wouldn't speak to me, wouldn't look at me, because she said I would corrupt her son. Corrupt her son! He was out there screwing his brains out. But me? I was a Hollywood Hussy, an evil actress.

I guess it's a common misconception that actresses are "fast." This happened to me when I was in New York. I still weighed two hundred and forty pounds, before I lost weight. And I took a Christmas job—I read about it in *Backstage* magazine—selling a toy called Copy Fun. It couldn't miss; you worked on commission, because you sold so many you could retire. But they only had an opening in White Plains. So I had to take the train from Manhattan up to White Plains every day.

And what was it, this marvelous toy? It was a piece of waxed paper and a tongue depressor. Now, there were no Game Boys back then, but trust me, there were more exciting things around than waxed paper and a tongue depressor. So business was a bit slow. And all I did was eat chocolate all day; my stand was right next to one of those Lindt chocolate places. I spent what few commissions I made on chocolate bars as big as my head. And one day I missed that damn train, and a very charming-looking collegiate guy picked me up. I can't believe I let him, but he looked so normal, and I guess I thought he was going to be interested in me. So he's driving along, and he says, "What do you do?"

"Well," I say, "I'm an actress, but right now I'm selling Copy Fun at Macy's in White Plains."

"So," he says, "you ever thought of doing porno?"

I said, "Excuse me?"

He said, "Yeah, you know, there's a lot of guys who like 'em big and beefy."

I said I wasn't aware of that, I didn't think that was my cup of tea, but thanks anyway. Unfortunately, I'd told him my name and I was listed, so he started calling me up all the time: "Now, are you sure? I've got some good movies here." You can't imagine; he looked like Brad Pitt. I mean, he looked so

Collegiate, Joe College...

Summer 1982

Dear Michael,

Well, you would be shocked, nay, appalled, by your former direc-tor, Madame Lubitsch. The Somers woman and I are now acting together in The Supporting Cast. *(The producer, who said he got my phone number from Jean Stapleton's dentist, said to me, "We're so thrilled to have you at our theater. Can you get us another semi-name?") And so I did.*

Anyway, her behavior on stage is despicable. Upon arriving, she told me that she would act me off the stage. I did not realize, however, that she intended to accomplish this by never letting another actor speak. Call me crazy; I kind of like to learn my lines and my cues, but I guess that's not right for everybody. She is playing her part of Mae as if she had St. Vitus' Dance. (Now, I'm not sure if that's a two-step or a disease, but you get the idea.) I said, "Thank god Michael Bell is not here to see this."

Things are pretty rustic here. It's a lovely resort area that makes Coney Island look like the French Riviera. I arrived to summer in New England, something I had heard more than enough about from Brett, only to discover it was forty degrees and everybody here was just like her: bossy and eccentric.

I had been told it was a beach town; what it is is four thousand rocks and a foot of sand, and damp. I was ushered to my fabulous

accommodations, the Reef Motel, with its ocean view (were it not for this six-foot lime green sea wall). You could, of course, hear the ocean, but I have a lovely record of the ocean in L.A., where a person's panty-hose dry in something less than six and one-half days.

As for the structure itself, it's right out of Psycho. I know I've said it before, but this time I am staying in the definitive Norman Bates Memorial Suite. One doesn't have to worry about being stabbed in the shower by Tony Perkins, as one could hear him coming, because he'd have bronchitis and would be seriously coughing.

Things perked up as I began an affair with my co-star and acting, two of my favorite summer pastimes. You know what the Somers woman always says: "There are only two things to do on the road, shop or screw, and you can always tell by the condition of one's wardrobe which one you picked." I do seem to turn into Paprika the Gypsy Trollop on the road.

Anyway, Joe is a lovely guy with only one small quirk. Aside from his Father Murphy fantasies, which I myself liked quite a lot, he likes to join hands before each performance and call upon the spirit of all the actors who ever lived to join in our experience. Now, hon, you know me—I'll take all the help I can get, dead actors included, but here's the thing: there's no guarantee that some of them dead "bad" actors might not sneak on with us, and that I don't need. One night we had the spirit of Keefe Brasselle.

You know, it occurs to me it's a wonder I ever get laid, what with my back that goes out, my clogged sinuses, my vaporizer, my European beauty mask, my chiropractic pillow... One morning I turned over seductively, wearing my black sleep mask, and he said, "Oh, good, I always wanted to f**k the Lone Ranger."

It's New England and I've had my picture taken with more fish, dead and alive, than you can shake a stick at. Here I'd gone through my entire life and never had anyone say to me "Smile and lower your lobster." Jesus, I thought I was back in David Craig's class. Well, I guess he was right. If that lobster isn't doing anything, get it down below that *nipple line. Actually, good advice when dealing with a live lobster, anyway.*

I'm going to New York for a while after closing here, and plan to start laying the groundwork for my upcoming career in the musical theater. I first plan to check out the possibility of replacing Jennifer Holliday in Dreamgirls, *since that woman stopped me on the street screaming, "Oh, god, it's you! Everybody says I look just like you!" and she was six feet two and black.*

Love,

Marcia

I was still in therapy with my wonderful Frederick during all of this, so as each of these relationships would bite the dust, I would drag them to Frederick and I'd say, "He's going to miss me," and Frederick would say, "Read my lips! He's thrilled to get away from you! Don't you understand? You're out of their league. You've got to move on." But when somebody tells you, "I don't want a relationship; I'm too damaged. But if I did want one, I'd want it with you," well, that's very seductive. And that's what Marvin said to me when I dragged *him* to Frederick. That, among other things. But let me tell you about Marvin from the beginning.

Marvin, I thought, was a step up. My "creep-o-meter" must have been on the blink. Of course, he looked pretty good that first day. And a lawyer, bound to be smart and successful. Wrong. Do you know forty-five percent of all the lawyers in the U.S. live in California? And I find the one who's broke and unsuccessful. And a dope smoker. Smoked dope *all* the time. And was *reeeal* angry. And lookswise, another not-Tom-Cruise who was constantly finding fault with me. But when I met him, I thought he was at least Mr. Close.

The highlight came when I was invited to Bob and Ginny Newhart's twentieth anniversary party, and he went with me. He was so drunk and stoned—I've never seen anybody outside of a Three Stooges movie do this—he literally fell into his mashed potatoes, like this: Wump. Face down, directly into his food. Of course, the Newharts and their guests didn't blink; they were all used to the people I showed up with. No wonder they were happy for me on my wedding day! No wonder!

I never drank at all back then. I took Marvin home and put him to bed. He woke up just enraged at me, and he said, "Don't you dare ever tell anybody." Well, this was worrisome; he should have been kissing my ass "till it barked like a fox," as Brett says. He should have been just incredibly apologetic. But he wasn't; he was furious. Anyway, I told a mutual friend what had happened because I was concerned—did he have a drinking problem? Does he have a drinking problem? And I said, "Please, you must not say anything." Well, she went right to him. So he came to me angry beyond belief, and said, "You've betrayed me and I don't want to see you ever again. Get away from me."

But I kept thinking, "I can make this go; I can make this move forward. *I can make my mother love me and my father stop beating me up.*" But he was so hateful. And also he hated my animals. He just hated them. So Maggie, my beloved and elderly border collie, pooped in his shoe. She pooped in his shoes; she peed on his briefcase. The more he hated her, the more she pooped and peed on him. If somebody said to me now "I don't like your animals" or "I don't like your kid," it would be goodbye and good luck. But back then I wanted so badly for it to work out with Marvin. Go know. I convinced him to come see Fred with me—a couples' therapy session—and what Marvin said was, "She was good in bed, but I never loved her."

The horrible thing is, the night he dumped me, he wanted to have sex, and I did. I did. The guy says "Uh, I don't want to see you again, you're not for me, but let's have one more roll in the hay." *And I did.* Pathetic, isn't it? I sold myself short for a very long time. Then he says, "Come on, I'll buy you dinner." *And I went.* And cried all through dinner, still managing to devour an appetizer, entrée, and dessert. I cried and cried and cried.

Next I became a Buddhist. I started chanting to attract people, men especially, who would appreciate me. I no longer wanted to be the recipient of the Zelda Fitzgerald Emotional Maturity Award.

It didn't happen overnight, but I began to grow up a little and no longer felt that I needed a man to be happy. Chanting did that for me; it really opened a door. It opened the door for my wonderful Denny.

7 don't look back

→

I Got Rhythm

When I had hit forty, I decided to celebrate by doing something that was hard for me. I had been wanting to sing for some time, so I started studying with David Craig. I'd been hearing about him from his wife Nancy Walker. She was in *Rhoda*, which taped right next door to *The Bob Newhart Show*. I had signed up for him once before, but he was just too formidable and I quit. But I *really* wanted to sing.

Those first few weeks in David's class were just awful. Much later David said to me—he was very grand—he said, "Mahsh," (he used to call me Mahsh; he never used r's) he said, "Mahsh, you know how fond I am of you, but Mahsh, those first few weeks were a nightmare. But you were very brave. Because people knew who you were."

I remember the first day; he made everybody sing "Where or When" to kind of get a bead on us all. I was so terrified that I never blinked, and I "typed" the words to the song. My fingers were flying at my sides. I remember Carrie Fisher came that day to observe, and after I finished, she ran from the room. I don't know if there's any connection. There was this great silence at the end. And David said, "Well, Mahsh, how do you feel?"

And I said, "I think I'm giving a very good impression of a woman who is conscious."

But I've always had more guts than brains, and I just kept trying. And David would say, "Well, Mahsh, I think we've worked our way up to bus and truck. Not national company yet, but perhaps bus and truck."

After I'd been with him for a while, I had an audition in New York for *42nd Street*, and I called him afterwards: "David, it was the most wonderful thing, the experience of my life, and it was fabulous; it was."

And he said, "Really, Mahsh? What did they say?"

"They said . . . they said, '*Thank you.*'"

There was a short silence, and then he said, "Well, Mahsh, isn't that nice? I'm so happy for you."

David was a most extraordinary teacher. His students adored him and his pianist and assistant, Gary Carver. He used to get furious with people who tried to tell him how much he meant to them. He always insisted that when he died he didn't want a memorial service, because, he said, "I don't want people I can't remember and never liked anyway up there talking about how I changed their life. *It's just a class.*"

But it wasn't. Because in a business where you are always hearing you're too old, you're too fat, you're too young, you're too thin, you're all wrong, this was a class about finding the best part of yourself. That's why a lot of people didn't stay, but that's why a lot of other people considered it a real life experience. No other teacher ever did what he did. Because he didn't want to teach just singing, it was singing for actors. He wasn't interested in your voice at all; it was about acting, singing and acting—it was a fabulous class. And now that he's gone, there's no one to pick up the slack. He taught an awful lot of stars, and he got an awful lot of stars ready for Broadway.

Now that I had triumphed in David Craig's class, I had a new goal: to get paid for singing. And this in spite of the fact that once I got up there and opened my mouth, it was clear I didn't know what I was doing. People used to run from the room crying after David's critique, but I never understood that, because for all of my neuroses, I never took personally what any director said to me. Unless he was real mean or something, I just thought, "I've got to listen. I've got a lot to learn here, and I've got to listen to these people." You know, this is a business where only fifteen percent make a living wage, and only six percent of all jobs go to women over forty. But I figured somebody has to be in that fifteen percent; somebody's got to be one of those women. The older I get, the more I respect my strong points. And in that class, my strengths certainly held me in good stead, because I just hung in there and kept trying.

So I'm singing there and I'm thinking, this is it, I've got to get paid for this. All around me people were much better than me, the class would applaud for them and everything, and sort of look the other way when I sang, but I kept plugging away.

Then somebody told me about a guy who worked at the Sacramento Music Circus. I called him up and I said, "You don't know me, but I'm a friend of a friend, and I want to sing onstage there." His name was Leland Ball, and we met, and he hired me to do *Gypsy* up in Sacramento. I once did a production of *The Music Man* in Fairfield, Iowa, in 1962, and it was wonderful. Every once in a while everything falls together, and it's magic. It doesn't have to happen on Broadway; it can happen in your backyard. We've all seen it happen. And that happened in the field house in Fairfield, Iowa, and it happened again in the round in this 120-degree heat in this tent in Sacramento. I played Tessie Tura, and it was magical.

July 16, 1983

Dear Sher,

Well, I started this summer with a broken heart and two dead dogs, and I just finished my musical comedy debut in a tent in beautiful downtown Sacramento. It was fabulous. I wish you'd seen me as Tessie Tura. I wish somebody who loved me had seen me; I was adorable.

There I was, singing and dancing and bumping and grinding and laughing and scratching, and luckily I was on stage at the time. I'm forty years old and I'm in the musical theater. God, I'm a thrilled woman. And the reviews weren't bad at all. They said I was fine or just right or terrific, but not one of them said, "Get that woman out of the musical theater."

Our star, Jo Anne Worley, is doing Gypsy *again in Long Beach in February and wants me to do it with her. Of course, none of it means dick, but read my lips: I'm not through with singing. I've decided never to go anyplace without an orchestra, which will complicate dating and traveling. However, I'm sure I'll never have another date again, so that should be no problem.*

Fast-forward to my next gig, The Prisoner of Second Avenue *with Corbett Monica in beautiful downtown Ivorytown, Connecticut. What a drag. I mean, where's my orchestra? Where's my conductor? Where's my choreographer? Where's my bell tone? I want to ride that sting and mount that song. Here I am in this dreary production in a hotel room with no TV, no phone, a smelly rug and a mattress that's about six months younger than I am. Sure, sure, it has the ocean, but this is a joke ocean here, barely an oceanette. You have to walk out about two miles before it covers your ankles. I'm telling you, Norman Maine would have a hard time committing suicide here at the lovely Hahn's Motel and Car Wash.*

And not only is our director old, deaf, toothless, cranky, and hostile, he likes to do everybody's part, too. After he blocks a scene within an inch of its life and gives endless interpretation and line readings, he gets up there and does it for you (the part, thank god; the other would be more than the human spirit could bear). Then acts out the whole damn scene, plus does the preshow speech and sells brownies in the lobby (that's the dessert and not the little girls, but with this sleazo, you never know). I can't stand him; he's all over me like a tent and then treats his cast like shit.

I have been surrounded this summer by younger people (I hate that phrase, "young people") who have never heard of anyone I have ever mentioned, living or dead. There I was, talking to a group about Esther Williams, and they all just stared at me. After I began to shake visibly at the very thought that I was among people who will never see Esther do the backstroke, one of them, whom I now refer to as Miss Congeniality, said, "Listen, don't feel bad. We didn't know who you were, either."

Oh, well, que sera, sera, as our beloved Doris Day once put it.

Love from your "older" sister,

Marcia

So *Gypsy* was a huge hit up in Sacramento. Jo Anne Worley played Mama Rose. She and I had known each other as a couple of comedy gals in Hollywood, but we really hit it off doing *Gypsy* together. Jo Anne was a woman with a mission, and that mission was to fix me up. Her standards weren't that high; about all she asked was that he be breathing.

Towards the end of the run she had said, "You know, I'm going to do *Gypsy* in Long Beach, but I can't get you the part; you're going to have to audition."

The Best Decision of My Life

I drove down there, which took me about three hours. It was a real musical audition; they wanted me to dance and stuff. So I thought, "Well, I don't know; this doesn't look good for me." And the choreographer was rolling his eyes like, "Look who they've given me here! Look at this!" But somehow, because I did have the name, and I was willing to do it for a dollar and a half and a pack of Juicy Fruit, I got the part. Not much money, but they gave me an "Also Starring Marcia Wallace"; you know, one of those end credits in the boxes.

At this point, I was offered a sixty thousand dollar tour of a play up in Canada. But I was chanting every day and I just had a feeling I should take this Juicy Fruit job instead, because I really wanted to sing. So I did. Once again I thank my lucky chickens.

The theater we were playing at was the Long Beach Civic Light

Opera, and the offices were housed at the Breakers Hotel. Jo Anne and I were down there doing a radio interview with some thirteen-year-old girl who had a radio show in her basement or something. And this terribly handsome man comes up to me and says, "Miss Wallace, I'm sure you don't remember me. My name is Dennis Hawley, and we met many years ago when I was working in the Stanford Court Hotel in San Francisco. I came up and told you I was a fan of yours."

And I'm sure, given my natural bent for flirtatiousness and charm, I said, "Oh, yeah? I don't remember."

But Jo Anne said, "Who was that? Who was that?"

"He's the general manager of the hotel," I said, "and I guess I met him once." And we both looked at him and we both thought, "Nah, no way. Too cute. He can't possibly be available." So we went on. But one of the producers at the Long Beach Civic Light Opera decided that Dennis would be somebody good for me to meet. It never occurred to me. I thought it couldn't be possible, this cute guy interested in me, so I just said, "Fine, Peggy. Whatever."

He was supposed to come to the opening night party, and we were supposed to go out afterwards. But I got stuck backstage, and I didn't make it to the party for an hour and a half, and he was gone. So Peggy gets on the phone and calls him up, and he says, "Oh, I'm sorry, it's not going to work for me tonight." Much later I understood that if Dennis is in his jammies, in his bed, he's not getting up. "I'm sorry it didn't work out. I waited a long time, and I just didn't know what had happened."

So I thought, "I can't even get fixed up right! I'm never going to meet anybody. I'm never going to find anybody. Just let it go!" And I remember being real steamed.

But I was staying in the hotel, because we had a matinee the next day. And when I woke up in the morning a note had been slipped under my door, in the best penmanship I'd ever seen: "Dear Miss Wallace, I'm honored to have you in my hotel. I saw you—your performance was great, your butterfly was a smash, I'd love to take you to dinner. How may I contact you? Sincerely, Dennis Hawley."

And then he sent up breakfast, and then he sent up flowers. And I literally almost broke my neck getting to the phone.

But he was very smart; he'd left the building. All of this was on a Sunday. And he didn't call me back till Tuesday. It was a long wait. But finally he called, and I remember sitting in the bedroom in my old house talking to him on the phone. I was kind of witty: "Well, Long Beach. I'd never been to Long Beach, but you know what they call it? They call it Iowa by the Sea. Hah, hah, hah." Lots of hollow ha-ha-has. So he said, "How about we go to dinner?" I didn't realize then how he liked to eat early and be in bed early. I said, "Well, you know I have the show, how about afterwards?" and he said, "How about 4:30 or 5:00?"

He got a friend to open up his restaurant early. It was called the Grotto or something. It was right across the street from the theater, and of course anyone in their right mind would just have eaten a sprig of lettuce or two. I mean, I had to put on my stripper costume, for god's sake. But that was the night that started our incredible appetite together for everything. And we ate and we ate and we drank and we drank and I can't believe I ever got into my costume. But I did, and I just sort of lumbered onstage. And I was a woman smitten; absolutely smitten. And he was, too, but I could tell he was nervous. Nobody had ever been nervous over me; I'd met him in the bar of the Breakers, and I could see he was nervous. But we just had the best time that night, talked and ate, talked and ate.

The next day we spoke, and he said, "Why don't you bring some of the people over from the cast, and we can do a little party in the restaurant?"

So I did, and then of course Jo Anne started with her wedding cake number; she was just relentless. But Dennis was charming and adorable, and everybody thought he was, well, charming and adorable. Then the next night, I remember a couple of other people came to the show, and I was dying for them to meet him, but he said he wasn't available that night, and I realized he had been up late so many nights he was exhausted.

Then the play closed, and I would have no more reason to be in Long Beach.

I didn't consider myself a promiscuous gal, having gone years without sex, but when I met somebody I liked I was not one for waiting too long. This time, though, I thought, "God, better calm down here. No matter how attracted you are to this guy, you've got to calm down. Take your time. Get to be friends, miss; don't be flinging your dress over your head." Our next date, he picked me up. We were supposed to go to a play in La Mirada, and then somehow we both realized we didn't want to do that, and we turned around, and he said, "Let's go to the Queen Mary." That's they famous ocean liner they docked in Long Beach and turned into a hotel. So we had a great dinner on the Queen Mary, and we went back to one of the endless rooms at the Breakers. But this wasn't right for him. I could tell this was throwing him for a loop too much, and my flinging my dress over my head didn't help at all. He said, "I've got a night off. We'll have a real date. I'll come; I'll cook dinner at your house. This has got to be right." Such an unbelievably classy guy.

And he drove up that next Tuesday. At that time, I lived way up in the hills, and he got wildly lost and called me from a drugstore, and I said, "Stay there; I'll come get you," and then I couldn't find him, and we're both wandering around this huge drugstore parking lot calling out each other's names, and finally we connected, and he followed me up to the house, and by this time, we were starving, and he threw together a delicious omelette and we ate and laughed and talked, and that was the night that began our incredible love affair. And from the very beginning it was just the easiest thing in the world. After all those years of anguish and everything being too hard, it was just magical.

8 don't look back

→

...I Got My Man

I don't know if he started out by saying he didn't want to get married. You know me, hon—I was just grilling him about his life, as I do to everyone. He'd gone with this woman for nine years, and then they were married for nine months, and he wanted out so bad that he got himself drafted during the Vietnam days—that's how bad he wanted out of the marriage. So he ran screaming into the night from the first Mrs. Hawley, and into the army in the late sixties for a year.

Now, Dennis, I imagine, would take to the army about like I would. It's clear in my case; anybody who knows me knows that I hate to be told what to do. But you don't know that about Dennis at first, because he appears so flexible, and he'll listen to you, and he'll appear to be very agreeable—and then he goes right on and does exactly what he wants to do. So he hated and despised the army with his whole being. And he firmly believed, he told me later, that if he went to Vietnam he'd be killed. So what he did, with his organizational skills and his charm and his intelligence, he made himself indispensable to some sergeant. And the sergeant said, "I've got to keep this guy here; he's running this office." So they never sent him to Vietnam. Later on he told me that the sergeant dressed up in drag every Saturday night; the officers held many a cross-dressing gala. So much for "Don't ask, don't tell."

He got out after a year around '69 or '70 and started traveling around the country in the hotel biz. He worked in San Francisco at the Stanford Court for about six years, then went to Boston to work at the Parker House and the Colonade. In 1982, he got a position as general manager of the Breakers Hotel in Long Beach. Two years later he met me. Our first date was March 1, 1984.

At that time his older brother was staying with him. He came for two weeks and had been there a year. Dennis told me that "Tom is just a little on the paranoid side." Jeez, I guess so. Our first conversation went something like this: "Hi, I'm Marcia."

"I'm Tom, Dennis's brother. You know, God told me all women are sluts."

"Uh, really?" I said.

"Well, what can I tell you?" he said. "God told me all this."

And I—talk about your exercise in futility—would argue with him: "Isn't it amazing God created all these people, but he doesn't like any of them?"

"Well, hey," he said, "I'm only the messenger. I only tell you what God tells me. You can't trust women."

I just finished Wally Lamb's novel *I Know What You Want*, about schizophrenic twins, and I suddenly realized that Tom was a tragic figure. Prior to the onset of his symptoms, he was a popular and successful guy, a great teacher, a loving husband and father. And then it all turned, and of course he refused to take medication, and spent the rest of his life alienated from his family who loved him so much. And I was wrong; I should never have baited him so much. Dennis used to tell me, "Please don't try to argue with him; don't try to reason with him." I remember the first time Dennis got mad at me. I said something kind of nasty about Tom, and he said, "Marcia, that's my brother." He was very protective; he was very good to his family.

I thought his family would be thrilled to meet me, but none of them were, I guess for a variety of reasons. The very first time I met his parents, I was so eager, and I said, "I'm so happy to meet you;

I'm just crazy about your son." And his mother said, "Well, we all are, Marcia; we all are." But I was so happy I never paid any attention to it.

His parents used to come out and stay with him for two or three months of the year in these hotels and get room service and everything; oh, the perks were great. The salary sucked and the benefits sucked, but being a hotel manager had great perks. He was living at the hotel. His brother worked nights, and then they got an apartment with two bedrooms. I remember one time in our passion of the moment I decided to go down there with my fur coat on and nothing else. And that was the night that there seemed to be eight hundred doormen on duty; every time I turned around, someone else wanted to take my arm and lead me somewhere. I kept saying, "Fine! I'm fine!" I finally got to his apartment and opened the door and flashed him. Of course that's the moment his brother walks in. Oh, it was just hilarious.

But it got sticky with Tom because he really was mentally ill. He wasn't happy to see me there, and it put Dennis in a difficult position. And everybody hated my dogs. The good dogs, the dogs I loved, were dead. These were the second team; I wasn't that crazy about them myself. One day Tom got upset and he moved out of the apartment. This was fine with me, but for the first time in my life, I shut up. Perhaps not everyone wanted my opinion. I don't know if I would have been able to without my practice of Buddhism, the clarity and wisdom it brought out in me.

Years later, I was trying to tell my son about this concept—the thing that if I can do it, I'm happy, and if I can't do it, I suffer most—which is to try and appreciate what I have, and not concentrate on what I don't have. In the past, I'd try to beat life into those relationships—*he won't and he won't and he won't*—and I was always miserable. Now, I was ready to enjoy what I had and not worry about Dennis's unwillingness to get married.

I'd Beat the Horse; Denny Would Cook It

As I've said a million times, Dennis and I had the plus of being in the right place at the right time, both of us ready for something, both mature, both having experienced life, both having been through a lot—but we had no baggage. The chances of being forty and having no ex-spouses and no kids is very rare; it almost never happens.

We had a tremendous amount in common, but it's not that we didn't have our differences. There was negotiation to be done. But we got to the same place at the same time. And for once I wasn't beating that poor old dead horse. Just let him rest. Because I had attracted someone who appreciated me, and thought I was just swell.

Love, Families and Vacuums

Dennis was in the hotel business, don't forget. He wanted to create an environment where people were comfortable. He loved things to look good. He loved beauty and symmetry and design. He loved good food, he loved good houses, he loved good furniture, he loved good times. He was also extremely well-organized. *My* organizational skills leave something to be desired. Once, when I had to move my couch (after my house caught fire—stay tuned), I found my will and two lizards. I guess the cat had brought them in (the lizards, not my will). Although I do believe it's a good idea; I still file all my important papers under the couch.

So even though Dennis had a place for everything and everything in its place, I didn't know where the place was. I didn't know where *my* place was. And after he moved in with me, not a day went by that I didn't have to call him up and ask him where stuff was. It's just that I would come in the house, I'd be in the kitchen, I'd get distracted, and that's why I ended up finding an avocado in the sock drawer, for example, or Tupperware in the shower. But he learned to be little less organized, and I really tried harder. I'd clean the kitchen and I'd stand there so proud: "Is this good or what?" And he'd say,

"Oh, honey, that's so good! Look how clean everything is!" And the next thing I knew, he'd get his little sponge out. But he never made me feel that I was failing, or that my efforts weren't good enough. What he did, he did with humor. "You know me, honey—some people believe in fairies; I vacuum." He *liked* to iron!

Now, I don't want you think that I was some sort of slattern. I mean, I'd get the laundry, and certainly I cleaned up after he cooked, because he did the cooking. Well, I came to this marriage knowing how to cook five dishes. All of which were extremely high in fat content. My famous one being Party Chicken, which was chicken breasts wrapped in bacon, lying on ham, covered with sour cream and mushroom soup and cheese. Tasty, but you could feel your arteries hardening even as you chewed. (Come on over, hon—I'll cook my Party Chicken, and then we'll have a nice heart attack.) Oh, yes, and there was Thanksgiving dinner with my Party Turkey. I had this trick where you dipped the dishtowel in peanut oil and then covered the turkey with it so the nice juice would seep down. And then one year I couldn't find my dishtowel so I used a red one, and we had red juice. And that's when he said, "Honey, would you be very upset if I did the Thanksgiving dinner from now on?" And I thought to myself, "Hmm . . . should I be mad?" And then I thought, "What, are you crazy? *Are you crazy?*"

He wasn't some sort of obsessive person who ran around and made the bed when you got up to go to the bathroom. He just very casually, very calmly made the house a wonderful, warm, beautiful, loving place to be.

Now, we also had to do some negotiation on talking. Because I felt you just couldn't talk enough about things. Springing from the "beat the dead horse" school of life. And I was always getting verbal— but not necessarily articulate—when I was upset. I could see his eyes—sort of, "Here she comes again. Oh, god, she wants to have a talk." But he learned to talk more, and I realized that I could actually have an unuttered thought. I didn't have to share every single thing that whizzed through my mind.

Because we were so right together, and because we had such love, passion, affection, respect and enjoyment of each other, none of this ever seemed as hard as back in the days when I was trying to make a relationship happen with those guys who didn't even *like me to begin with.*

I'd always been a very passionate gal. But this was the first time I'd ever had this wonderful thing: a sex life with somebody that I trusted. Well! This was something totally new for me. And great fun. I got to be even more like Paprika the Gypsy Trollop. (My friend Natalie Bates told me about a book she'd read, all about fat being a feminist issue. I was very interested because we both still struggled with our weight and everything. She said very seriously that she would give it to me, and that it would change my life. When I opened the package there was this hilarious dime novel from the forties called *Paprika the Gypsy Trollop.* Which was pretty much me. Flipped that dress over her head, and went through her life that way. Fat had nothing to do with anything. Right away I took Paprika as my role model.)

Get Them Guys in Hospitality

So Denny and I had great fun and great times. I couldn't get enough of this fabulous guy, and we couldn't keep our hands off each other; we played the Shepherd and the Pizza Waitress, you know, and the Rabbi and the Rockette. It was just fabulous.

But back to the subject of negotiation, we did have some problems with animals. When he said he liked animals, I thought he liked animals like I do. But not very many people do, actually. He and Mikey picked out the fabulous Bingo as a puppy. And then when Bingo had eaten a great many pieces of Denny's clothing, Denny wanted to get rid of him. I said, "Well it was your idea to get this puppy," and he said, "I made a mistake!" (This is what was so great about him: "Hey, I made mistake.")

I don't give away animals, so we kept Bingo, and eventually Denny loved him, too. Denny was such a great role model for a son.

Because Denny had not an ounce of arrogance, or showing off, or machismo; just a great sense of himself and comfort in his own skin. And confidence in who he was.

There was one time when he left the Breakers Hotel and the guy who came in after him screwed up, and they tried to blame Dennis for all that was wrong, and I said, "Boy, doesn't that steam you?" And he said, "No, I know what I do. I know what I'm worth."

He would sometimes say a funny thing to me in my ear, and I'd want to repeat it to everyone immediately, because whenever *I've* said anything funny I'd practically want to hire a skywriter lest someone wouldn't hear my fabulous remark. But he didn't care. He just didn't care; he didn't have that kind of ego. And people were drawn to him because of that, because he was just such a swell guy and a gentleman. Such a gentleman.

But anyway, back to animals. He did like the animals, in a way, and he even let them in his bed from time to time. But plucking cat hair out of the butter was not his idea of heaven. That was almost a deal-breaker.

I didn't see why it was a problem, but he said, "Work with me on this." So we did. When we got married, we still had the fabulous Dr. Pepper, a toy poodle and one of the foulest animals ever. Denny used to say, "Why don't you find a home for this dog?" I would say, "Oh, let me see. Let me write the ad now: Old, crappy, hateful, mean, smelly dog with open sores needs loving home." Oh, sure, that phone'll start ringing immediately. So Denny put up with him. He put up with a lot.

Order Meets Chaos

I was so cluttered; there was always the chance that you might find Jimmy Hoffa buried somewhere in the stuff I had on top of my refrigerator. And my car—once in a while, when Denny drove my car, he would get his Dustbuster out, clean the car and put everything in the trunk. But it was never like, "Dammit, clean out this car! I don't want to drive this car!" He just said, "Hey, it's important to me. I'd like to have this stuff put away. Okay by you? And I said, "Sure, what do I care?" Of course, the minute I got back in the car all that stuff started to reproduce itself; it looked like a family of four lived in my back seat. So it's good that we had our own cars.

But like I said, it was never any sort of obsession, and he never made you feel like it wasn't your house. We'd also fight from time to time about driving because he said I was bossy. I suppose that's true. Many of my women friends are much bossier than I am. I've never had much luck bossing people, and I didn't have any luck bossing him, but that didn't stop me from trying.

He was the sweetest guy in the world. But strong. He would listen to me tell him what I thought and what I wanted him to do, listen with grave interest, pat me on the arm, and then go right ahead and continue doing what he wanted. But in terms of the driving, he usually gave in and let me drive. "Life is too short," he said. Probably because most of the time when he drove us, we would get lost. We would drive, like, two thousand miles, and then he would get us lost in the last hundred yards; he couldn't find our house.

Somehow we always had a great time. The best time of all was when we were courting and he had the hotel. Two hundred and fifty rooms! We just went from one room to the other, made love, rented movies, had room service—it was just unbelievable. My memory always comes back to that time. We talked and laughed and loved.

We never lived together until a couple of months before we got married. And by that time, I'm sure there were moments when he thought, "Uh, is she going to shut up? She's driving me crazy." And he couldn't take it if he thought I was being cruel or if I got really scared, as I would get sometimes, and go on and on. "I don't deserve this treatment," he would say. So I learned that he had his boundaries. And most importantly I learned that this was a guy who deserved respect, because he was so respectful of me. From the time our son was born, if he felt Mikey was disrespectful to me in any way, he would say, "That's your mother. That's your *mother!*" I wish I had recorded that voice. I'd play it now.

So we got to be like kids, but without having to *be* kids. We had a couple of bucks and we had some experience and we got to do what we wanted. He seemed to be totally committed to me; he wasn't interested in seeing anybody else. He wanted intimacy, so it wasn't a question of him not wanting to get close. He wanted to do everything, but he didn't want to get married. But he said, "Let's go to Europe; neither one of us has ever been to Europe."

So off we went and it was wonderful. We were there for almost a month. I don't know if I could go back, I really don't, because it was so perfect. Going to the wine country. London, Paris, Venice, Florence, Rome. We took the trains all over Europe. At one point we went to the Moët Chateau in Epernege where Dennis knew someone. It's hard to believe it was still during that time when people just couldn't handle that we weren't married. And this poor woman who was in charge there kept trying to make it all right: "This is Mr. Forster, and this is Mr. and Mrs.—Mr., Mr. and Mrs. Wall—Mr. Hawley." And I thought, "My goodness, they've got to catch up."

I picked a fight in Rome, right before we came home. He said, "Oh, boy, I'll be glad to get home." And I was livid: "How dare you! You want to get away from me! *I* could stay here forever!" He said, "I'm going to lie down now." And that's when I went out on my own and saw the Coliseum, the Catacombs and all that. Which is always the kind of gal I've been, and that's a good thing, too. We made up, of course, and everything was blissful again.

But we got back home (this was May of 1985) and I remember we were sitting up in the Skyroom in the Breakers, and he said, "Marcia, this was glorious, and I didn't know if we could be together for a whole month, and I discovered that we could. I loved it, but I gotta tell you, I still don't want to get married. I don't want to be with anybody but you, but I don't want a wife. I had a wife and I wasn't happy."

In my head, I was going, "But, but, but, you have to. We have to. I can make this happen." Instead, I shut up. I thought, "Just concentrate on what this guy's doing for you," which was plenty. We were having a magical love affair, he wasn't interested in anyone else, he wanted to be close, he wanted to be with me. Probably his biggest adjustment was to my messiness. He was so incredibly fastidious. But he'd negotiate a little bit: "Can we take the stuff off the top of the counter here, in case we find the Lindbergh baby underneath?"

I'd go down to Long Beach on the weekends; we'd stay in the hotel and get room service. And sometimes we'd travel. There were hotels in Palm Springs. We went to Santa Barbara; we drove up the coast to Big Sur, then San Francisco, because he had all these friends in all these hotels where we could stay.

As it turned out, I only had to shut up for about six months. We got back from Europe in May of 1985 and we continued to just have this wonderful time. God, we had fun. We had six unbelievably spectacular years; everything about it was just wonderful. Unconditional positive regard, incredible intimacy and communication, passion— Dennis and I brought out the very best in each other. We really did.

We liked all the same things. Almost all. We both loved to travel, but we had different body clocks. He liked to go to bed early, and he liked to sleep a lot more than I do. But he stayed up a little later and I went to bed a little earlier. And he loved my independence. I'd been alone, a single woman, for most of my adult life, so I wasn't, "Well, if you don't go, I'm not going!" I'd go off and do my thing. And then he said, "Hey, I didn't know you were gonna be gone this much."

So I shut up in May, and in November, standing in my kitchen up on Appian Way, he said, "I can't go one more day without being married to you."

I just freaked, and I jumped up and down, yelling—I think I scared him—"Omigod! Omigod! Let's do it! Okay!" Next thing I know, we set a date. But three days later I was diagnosed with breast cancer.

9 don't look back

→

A Funny Thing Happened on the Way to the Altar

I found out about the cancer in what I thought at the time was a very weird way. I was lying in bed a couple of nights before Denny proposed, and I had a feeling something was up. I'd been getting regular mammograms—it's taken me years to pronounce that word. I've called it a mammiogram, a mammalgram; like Al Jolson's going to come to the door with a *ma-ammy-gram*! Maybe I couldn't say it right, but I was having them. I had had a mammogram about six months before, and insurancewise, wouldn't have been eligible for another one for quite some time.

Mammograms are the single most important tool women have; they can pick up something dangerous *years* before you can do it any other way. But nothing is one hundred percent reliable, and that's why women should use all the tools available: breast self-examination, a doctor's medical exam, and one more thing—gut instinct. I swear to you, hon, I had a feeling something was up. I thought at the time I'd be laughed out of the doctor's office, but since then I have met literally dozens of women who have shared similar experiences with me.

I met a woman recently who told me that when she was in her

fifties, she had a similar feeling—an intuition, a sixth sense, whatever you want to call it. She went to her doctor; he said "You're fine." She continued to feel that way. She went back; he said, "You're fine. You're getting on my nerves. You're fine." But she persisted; she felt that strongly. And sure enough, they did find a small malignancy, and she was there to tell me about it—in her eighties.

I also met a lovely woman of about thirty, who said, "I never used to give my health a minute's thought, not for one second. And then one morning I got in the shower and I knew; I knew in my deepest gut that I should go to the doctor." She did and was diagnosed with breast cancer, second stage. But if you think about it, it makes total sense, because we know our bodies better than anybody. We can feel from the inside out. And it's a win-win situation. Hey, if you're wrong, it was a false alarm; that's great. And if you're right, you will have gotten in there early enough.

As I say, I'd always been conscientious about my breast health and I had a feeling something was up. I mean, I couldn't really feel anything, but I figured, "What the hell? I'll go check it out." So I made an appointment. Then Denny proposed and I thought, "Things will be all right and I'm sure it's nothing and why don't I just cancel?" But I went anyway, and the doctor found the lump I wasn't sure was there. The mammogram showed that it was very small, less than a centimeter. Everyone was sure it was benign. My friend Caroline drove me to the clinic, because it was going to be a local anesthetic, where you don't go under. She stayed there while they removed the little lump. The doctors had said they would be able to tell in the operating room. Suddenly, everybody got very busy with their shoes, so I knew something was up. I was asking everyone, "What do you see? What do you see?"

It got real quiet and people were muttering, "No, no... your doctor will call."

Then I was home all alone and the phone rang, and the doctor said, "You don't have an appointment till next week, but I want you to come in tomorrow." I said, "Well, I want you to tell me on the phone."

"No, I can't tell you on the phone."

"I know it's bad news; you've got to tell me on the phone. I don't want to wait overnight not knowing what's going on."

He said, "You have breast cancer."

And I thought, "Well, I'm going to die." Because I had known women with breast cancer, and many of them had died. There's nothing like that diagnosis to make you feel out of control. Talk about the rug out from under you. You don't even feel sick, and somebody tells you you've got these mutant cancer cells running around in your body? It's totally natural, it makes total sense that you feel so thrown for a loop that you just want to turn it over to somebody: "Please, take care of it." Some authority figure. Some mommy-daddy-doctor. Please, take care of it.

But then I thought, "Well, dying can't be any scarier than the fear, the constant fear of death." So I thought, "I gotta move, here." Any action you can take makes you feel better. Working in partnership with your doctor. Any education. The Internet's amazing now; the life-to life contact. Moving forward makes you feel less scared, less impotent, less out of control.

The first thing my mother said was, "Is he still going to marry you now that you have cancer?"

The answer was yes, of course he wanted to marry me—more than ever.

I had thought my mother would be so happy when I told her I was getting married, but all she said when she met Denny was, "If only I were twenty years younger..." No "I'm so happy for you." It was only, "How could I get him for myself?" Ha, ha. She *loved* him!

She had met Denny that first Christmas. My dad was still alive. Dennis and I weren't even engaged yet, but all the parents were there and everything, both sets of parents. My dad was near the end, and his charm eluded Dennis. They never connected at all, which is too bad. But my mother certainly connected with Dennis. She used to come out to visit quite a bit, and he always put her up in the hotel. He was unbelievably generous to her.

The Hardest Words

When I was diagnosed, Denny made it very clear that he would love me without a breast if I had to have the surgery. I remembered a lovely woman who touched my life when I was about twelve. Virginia Evans was a wife and mother in my hometown, and she had breast cancer. She came to our house one day; my mother was giving her some clothing. I had occasion to see her without her clothes on, that extremely disfiguring scar from radical surgery. Much to my mother's chagrin—my mother was never so mortified—I said, "Boy, it must really be scary having cancer, huh?" And tears sprang to her eyes. She said, "You are twelve years old, and you are the first person to say the word to me." I was, but I somehow sensed her isolation and her loneliness.

Dennis went with me to see the doctor. Whenever I'm in a waiting room now, and I see a woman there with her loved one, I always think, "Great!" But then when the woman gets up and goes into the doctor's office alone, I want to say, "No, no, no! Go with her!" If there's ever a time when you need someone who cares deeply about your life by your side, that's it. But also, practically speaking, you're being assaulted by this news, all these new feelings and these strange words. Perhaps your loved one can think to ask a question that never occurred to you, or maybe even take notes. So when the doctor said, "You have breast cancer; I recommend a mastectomy," it was Dennis who said, "Well, tell me this: is there a difference in survival rate between a lumpectomy and a mastectomy?" The doctor said, "No, no, but if it were *my* wife..."

'Course, I was the one who said, "Well, what if it were your testicles?" But that's another story.

I still say that's a perfectly reasonable question, and you know what? There's no such thing as an unreasonable question. There's no such thing as a silly-waste-of-time question, a frivolous question. If any question you ask ever gets on your doctor's nerves, that should be it for him. Absolutely. Because it's *your* life and *your* body, and if you don't know the answer, you keep asking until you get it.

Dennis stayed with me. He went to every doctor's appointment; he went to everything. The only thing he couldn't do, for some reason, was wait at the hospital. He was never in one, until later. So he would drive me and then he'd leave. But then he'd come right back.

Before the actual surgery, I was in the hospital to check my axillary nodes. I ended up having to stay in a couple of days waiting for the result of the nodes. This is pre-HMOs; I'd have been kicked out the same day now. But the nodes were clean, and we talked about it and we did a lot of networking and a lot of researching, because I decided that no matter what they said, and despite the fact that I knew Dennis would love me with or without a breast, that I was a real good candidate for breast conservation. But it was also because I was planning a wedding at the same time. So that joy kept me confident. I meet women now who are so terrified during the whole process. But I had other things to do and to think about—my wedding!—so that was my good fortune, too.

When they removed the lump, the surgeon could tell right away it was cancerous. He cleaned out around it, did the margins and everything. Then he told me I had breast cancer and still recommended a mastectomy. But I opted for none, so I had radiation. And all it did, really, was make me tired. Like I said, I caught it early. I never got sick and it never came back. Now that's about a ten-minute movie-of-the-week, but it's plenty exciting for real life.

So my experience with cancer was about as good as it gets. The only way it would have been better would be if they'd said, "Hey, you don't have cancer."

Whenever I meet women who struggled with this twenty, thirty, forty, fifty years ago, those women are my heroes—the ones who didn't make it, the ones who did—when there was no networking, there was no support, there were certainly very few choices. You could lose your job, you could lose your insurance, and nobody said the word.

I had occasion to meet Mrs. Betty Ford, and she's always been a personal hero of mine. I think, twenty years later, it's hard to remember the impact of what she did. Nobody was saying the word "breast." Nobody was saying the word "cancer." They certainly weren't saying them together. And the wife of the president said, "Hello, I have breast cancer. Get a mammogram." Tens of thousands of women did, and the journey began.

It's hard for me to remember today what it was like when I was diagnosed in 1985. It was almost like the Dark Ages in terms of what's available in the way of treatment. They can build a breast in reconstructive surgery. They can do biopsies in twenty seconds in the room; you don't use that invasive procedure. There are cancer centers and comprehensive breast centers where women can find out within minutes instead of weeks what's going on. Imagine when a woman used to go have a mammogram, and then go back to her doctor, and then go for a chest x-ray, and a sonogram, and blood work—please, it could take weeks and weeks, and you could be so frightened by then, or so tired, that you just let it go. The way we combine everything now to work together for a diagnosis and treatment is definitely, definitely saving lives.

A Woman's Breast Is Close to Her Heart

When I was diagnosed, it was a ninety-seven percent mastectomy rate, very little lumpectomy. Change takes a long time for everybody. Like I said, I don't have any stock in lumpectomy; I don't get any kickbacks or anything. I know it's not for everybody. I know for some, their breast is too small, the lump's too big, there's calcification; sometimes a woman can't logistically do the necessary follow-up treatment. Sometimes she just doesn't feel safe keeping her breast in spite of the data. As for me, I thought, "If I can keep my breast, I won't have that constant reminder." So the feelings just run the gamut. I've met women who say, "Oh, please—take it," all the way to a young woman who said, "I'd rather die than lose my breast." Now, *that* absolutely breaks your heart. Nothing's more important than your life. I just want these choices to be a woman's choice, with nobody else's agenda.

I have a cousin who is a nun, and she had breast cancer. She was given one option: a mastectomy. Then she was reading later, something about breast conservation, and she said, "Oh, gee, I wonder why he didn't tell me about that?" And she went back to her doctor and asked, "Why didn't you tell me I could have saved my breast?" And her doctor, a perfectly nice guy, said, "Well, you're a nun." Not a bad guy, but he assumed that somehow, if we're not going to nurse a baby or be a topless dancer, we aren't entitled to keep our breasts if we'd like to. Hello? So I kind of have a pet peeve about this. These options should be available for everybody, no matter what their age; I want it to be the woman's choice.

So I made my choice. I ended up at one of the very first comprehensive breast centers in the country, and one of my cancer doctors was Monica Lewinsky's father. Yes, Clinton's girlfriend's father has seen my breasts. Thank you. You know how they're always telling you that there's six degrees of separation between each of us? Hon, there's only three degrees between my breast and Bill.

During this time, we were planning the wedding and still traveling back and forth between my house in the hills and the hotel in Long Beach. And having an unbelievably wonderful time. We rented movies and we took walks and we talked and talked and talked and talked and talked, made love, ate, traveled, I mean all the fun things there are, everything fun to do. And I've never been much of a phone gal, but he'd call me all the time. He would call me, not to check up, but just because he liked to talk to me, liked to check in.

We went back to his hometown shortly before we were married. There was a TV station in Detroit that had asked us to go on together, and for him to talk about being the partner of someone with cancer.

So we went back and he showed me the town where he grew up: Jackson, Michigan, a charming little town. His family was all there, including his younger brother, Doug.

Nobody ever said anything, but I felt from the get-go that I would not have been the Hawley family's choice for their beloved Dennis, and I'll grant you I wasn't exactly the girl next door, unless the girl next door was forty and opinionated. One of my favorite novels is *The Book Of Daniel* by E.L. Doctorow. A character in that book was described something like this: "It was the way he existed in the space he occupied—right out to the edges." I liked that. I always felt that way about myself, and I always hoped that was a good thing.

I may have been too much for a low-key family like the Hawleys. But I thought, "Hey, I at least have a shot here, warts and all," because Dennis's sister Suzanne (whom I love) had shaken things up quite a bit when she married a guy from Uganda. I guess I figured that if you live in a small town in the Midwest and your only daughter marries a guy from Uganda, you wouldn't mind if your son comes home with a Hollywood actress. Go know. It really hit the fan with Suzie's marriage, and the parents moved away to San Francisco. But I always admired them enormously because they soon decided that they did not want to be estranged from the daughter they loved, and when she had children, they moved back and became close again.

His parents seemed to move around a lot, following Dennis. By the time I met them they were retired. Max had been a foreman, a real kind of stoic. They were a family that held things inside. I think it was better to be in my family where we didn't hold anything in—we screamed and hollered and yelled and beat each other. (Well, maybe not.)

Denny adored his mother, Winifred. He worshipped her, and she him. (And read my lips on this one, girls, you do not want a man who doesn't love his mother; sew that into a sampler.) Anyway, his mother went through something that's always fascinated me, a situation similar to my mother's. I know what happened to my mother when my father went away. I was trying to explain this to Winifred. A whole group of young women in their twenties, their husbands went away—not for one year, like Vietnam; they were away in the war for two to four years. Most of them were strangers when they came back. Winifred made it sound like it was fine, just fine. But we've talked about it since, and she pretty much admits it was much harder. And they had the four kids, and seemed a very normal family, but all four kids were married twice.

Anyway, I didn't think Denny's mother liked me much, but my own mother didn't like me, so I was kind of used to it. I guess it was my karma, but because Denny liked me so much, it didn't matter until later down the line. My mother-in-law liked my sister best and my mother liked my sister best. I tried desperately to understand. I went to see a psychic and he said, "Your problem was that your life force was so strong, nobody ever knew what to do with you." I'd never thought of it that way, because I've always felt it was all the things I was *lacking* that made people not be able to handle me. Or be interested, or care about what I feared or dreamt. I think certainly growing up in the fifties, where denial was rampant and nobody talked about anything personal, somebody like me was very upsetting. My dad liked me, but I was just too much for the rest of them. And certainly too much for Denny's mother. But Denny said, "Don't you worry about it; I love you."

That's what was great about Denny. He would say, "You can loosen up. What do you care? They like you fine. I'm your family. Mikey and I are your family. We love you. Don't you worry; you've got us. What do you care?" And he used to say, "You brought life into my life. You're the life force of our family." But also he really calmed me down a lot. He was able to—how can I say this? I breathed more. I think what he gave me was love and breath. With Denny around, I never forgot to breathe, ever. And so I didn't worry about it. All I really wanted was for us all to be close.

10 don't look back

→

Our Love
Is Here to Stay

Our wedding was beyond words. It was the most wonderful wedding ever imagined. On May 18, l986, I married the man of my dreams at the Buddhist Temple in Cucamonga, California. I was indeed a blushing Buddhist bride.

First I have to tell you about Judy, crazy Judy Thomas. Judy was my manager, and agoraphobic; hated to leave her bed. She looked big and tough and a bit butch, and she had a very English, genteel sort of husband. And yet it goes to show you appearances are deceiving; they were madly in love with each other, and I adored them both. They gave us limos for the wedding party to the temple and then to the Breakers for the reception.

We had two hundred and fifty people. Denny was able to put everybody up at the hotel. I mean, we thought, "This is our wedding; we can do what we want. We don't have to scrimp." He said, "I want the best champagne." He felt that way; he just always wanted everything to be the best. So we hit our savings and had this great wedding. It *was*; just great. To this day, people come up to me and say it was the best wedding they ever went to.

But about Judy. She said to me, "Honey, I'm going in the first limo." There were four limos; I was in the second. And Judy was known to take a drink now and again, so she kept having to pee. And

Hubie Banks, the limo driver, kept getting off the freeway, and all the limos behind him would get off the freeway thinking we were there. Everybody's saying, "Do you know where Cucamonga is?" The drivers are all saying, "Do you know where Cucamonga is?" "No, but the lead driver, he knows, so don't worry." But I wasn't so sure.

Judy had to stop and pee three times. So here's this demented bride clawing at gas station bathroom doors: "Judy, I'm getting married. You've got to come out. *Come out!*" And all those people in those limos just looking baffled.

Now, we finally get there, and I discover that, unbeknownst to me, Judy had told some guy from the *National Enquirer* he could come and take pictures. So I had to scamper around and try and keep him away from Bob Newhart, because Bob was walking around looking very alarmed, and muttering, "Who is this guy? Who *is* this guy?"

My Uncle Jimmy walked me down the aisle. I wore white. Read my lips: *white.* I wore it and I looked fabulous. (If you can't look fabulous on your wedding day, you're in big trouble.) Finally the ceremony started. I've got a lot of photos of a lot of people rolling their eyes. The one regret I have, I wish I had thought to write out the San San Kudo ceremony in English, because people were saying, "Why isn't this in English?" The thing is, it was! The Buddhist priest spoke at us for a long time, and all I remember of the ceremony is, "Blide, gloom and fish." That's all I remember. "The blide and gloom are like fish." And I remember Dennis Dugan saying, "Aren't there consumer laws against a woman your age wearing white?"

I said, "To hell with it! It's my wedding day." When you get married at forty-three, you can wear what you want. And you can do what you want.

I had been in a million weddings as a kid where the bridesmaids have those awful dresses with those dyed-to-match pumps, and I thought, "Hey, I got me a great dress, my matrons (or whatever the hell they're called) can wear what they want." That's a great thing about being in a Buddhist ceremony; there're not a lot of rules about that.

Let Them Eat Cake

Okay, so my dad, who was not in good shape, didn't make it to the wedding. I knew he was on his way out if he passed up a wedding with stars. He was always in the wrong place at the wrong time. Once, the network was going to fly him in and put him on TV and surprise me, and there was the worst blizzard in the history of Iowa. That pretty much summed up his life: never in the right place at the right time. Finally passed the real-estate exam after thirteen flunks, and then the real estate market crashed. Now I finally get married and there's a free trip to L.A. and a fabulous party and stars, and he's too far gone to come. So my uncle Jimmy walked me down the aisle.

Denny and I loved music, and our favorite song was "Our Love Is Here To Stay." We loved all those old forties Gershwin songs. So we asked our friend Leslie Easterbrook to sing at the wedding. She came over one day so we could help her pick out the songs, and she sang a couple for us a cappella and it brought tears to our eyes, it was so lovely. Well, between then and the wedding, without saying anything to us, she decided she was too nervous to sing a cappella, she has to put it on tape and put a speaker in her ear. So of course she can't stop herself once she starts to sing. And so the day of the wedding, she's in the front, her tape is playing and she can't turn it off, she can't fast-forward or slow it down, and she's hitting the pew with her ring, hissing, "Come on! Come on! Where's the damn bride?" So I galloped down the aisle. I didn't even take my train with me. But I didn't care; I looked awful good. I looked beautiful!

And sweet Denny—I had told him how important it was to me to get married in a Buddhist ceremony, but he was worried. "Are you sure it's real? I mean, is this temple thing legal?"

I reassured him, and he said, "Well, then, once is fine by me."

But a lot of those Iowa people were absolutely mystified, rolling their eyes. There were plenty of people who loved it, though, who thought it was great. It *was* great. And I thought my Buddhist friend Bonnie Hamilton was wonderful that day, although I had an argument with her because she was trying to tell me my niece Kim couldn't pour the sake because she wasn't a Buddhist. Honestly! As if I was going to bump my niece! On my wedding day! My life force was pretty strong that day; I wasn't about to be talked out of much.

The reception was magical even though it was forty miles away. It was a long way for guests to travel from the temple to Denny's hotel. One guest said they hoped the marriage lasted longer than the drive. The food, the music, the arrangements—everything about it was perfect. People were so happy for us. After my history with men and everything, everybody loved Denny so much. And even though the wedding was perfect, everybody really had a great time because they were just so darn happy for us.

There was entertainment, wonderful entertainment by my friends. My friend Bryan Peterson got everybody up there to put on a show. Bob Newhart was hilarious: "I love a traditional Cucamonga-Long Beach wedding. I said to Ginnie today, 'Ginnie, let's go down to Long Beach.' We used to like to go somewhere every weekend, maybe West Covina, sometimes Pacoima. Today was Long Beach." People howled. It was like a Las Vegas show.

David Steinberg didn't want to go up on stage, and Brett said to him, "David, I'm from Canada, too, so get your little Jewish ass up here." And he was hilarious. He said when he was a kid growing up in Winnipeg, he had two dreams: one was to see Paris, the other was to attend a Buddhist wedding in Cucamonga.

Brett said, "The best thing about finding Mr. Right in your middle years? You don't have to worry about him going through a midlife crisis, because you're it." And Jo Anne Worley sang "I Don't Know Shit About Love," a song she and her husband Roger Perry wrote. Bobby Gorman sang "I Love to Cry at Weddings." And then that sweet guy that Dennis worked for, Mike Harrison, he got up and said, "We've heard a lot about Marcia, but we want you all to know she's getting about the best darn hotel man there is." The band was fabulous, too, and they had a great singer, Roeanne. Oh, god, she was good. And they would play anything.

A Buddhist friend did the videotaping, but he only talked to Buddhists, and the sound was off during the entire show. He missed Newhart; he didn't get anybody. And he was totally cavalier about it: "Oh, did I? Hmm." And he had called me and asked to be paid in advance. Imagine! Not going around to people I've known in my life, people I adored, and asking them to say something. I'm still pissed about it. I guess I'm not enlightened yet; that's weeks away.

At most weddings people stay a couple of hours, but at this one, they stayed and stayed and stayed; nobody left. And they ate the entire wedding cake; it was a strawberry cheesecake.

That night Denny and I stayed at the Hilton. They had given us the honeymoon suite; it had a Jacuzzi, and there was all this champagne. I don't know how anybody can stay awake on their wedding night, let alone do anything of a physical nature. We were just limp; with the champagne, in the hot tub, it's a wonder we didn't drown.

Fun Fun in Bora Bora

We didn't leave that morning for our honeymoon. Denny had all these great ideas: "Let's not be leaving the next day, because we'll be too tired." We got married on Sunday, and we didn't leave for our honeymoon till Tuesday.

Somebody had once told me something about Bora Bora, and it sounded fabulous. I guess we picked the most expensive place in the world, although when we were doing our major traveling back in '85, the dollar was so strong, we went to Europe for three weeks, and we bought tons of linen and glasses, and the whole trip was five thousand dollars. And that included everything hotels, food, trains, planes, everything we brought back. I guess now it's terribly expensive.

But about the honeymoon: I suggested Bora Bora, and he said, "Sounds good to me."

Bora Bora is an island. James Michener didn't call it paradise for nix, you know. It's surrounded by a lagoon, so there're never any storms. The winter temperature is 80 and the summer temperature is

82. You can bicycle all around the island; it's only seventeen miles. There's no phones or TV or anything.

The water is unbelievably clear, and the fish come right up to you. When you skin dive they come and take food out of your hands. And I'm a scuba diver, but the snorkeling was unbearably beautiful.

We rented a boat and captain, and he took us all around the island. He took us to a special place where you could ride manta rays; you could ride them! It was all manta rays and turtles. It was like a farm, and it was all fenced in somehow, right there in the ocean, in the lagoon. I thought at first that the manta rays would bite our hand off, but these were the non-problem ones. And the water! The visibility was about forty feet down, always. And there was a place you could snorkel with non-dangerous sharks.

The sea life just took your breath away. I snorkeled all the time, and Denny did too. But because we were never joined at the hip, sometimes he'd say, "I'm lying in this hammock today." And I'd go off and do what I wanted, snorkel a little bit or swim. And then we'd always meet and walk down to one of the restaurants. These were all grass huts with open walls and windows. And hammocks everywhere. There were hammocks in front of everyplace and hammocks by the water. The only thing was, the food all had to be shipped in from New Zealand, and it was terribly expensive, even then. They did have some local fish, and there were fruit trees and vegetable gardens. They grew everything. But for the hotels, a lot of stuff had to come in from New Zealand.

One night we were having a marvelous dinner at this wonderful little restaurant that was owned by a family. Everybody worked there, the grandma waited on you, and the kids bussed. Watching those kids, I brought up parenthood, and Denny said, "Marcia, I don't think I want kids."

And I knew to shut up.

11 don't look back

---→

Meant for Each Other

I had learned to keep my mouth shut, and I did.

We got married in May, and then in January, I did *The Odd Couple* with Jo Anne Worley down in Anaheim at the Grand Dinner Theater. Oh, we had the best time. Denny came down on the weekends, they gave us a hotel room with a Jacuzzi, and of course he and I spent my whole salary on room service. Unlike Jo Anne, who while she is a very generous person, when it comes to spending money, she has her own ideas. She would talk some guy out of his flat Andre champagne, and literally go through the dinner theater tables and find some old celery and a couple of stale crackers, and be in hog heaven. And Denny and I would be ordering meal after meal after meal after meal. We had a fabulous time.

Now all of this time I had never been using any birth control, and that seemed to be fine with Denny, I guess because I never got pregnant. He hadn't said anything more about having kids. But then . . .

Just like the wedding, on his own timetable, eight months after our last conversation about kids, he said he thought we should think about having a child. I tried for quite a while to get pregnant to no avail. We started to get real serious. He was checked and I was checked and there was absolutely no reason why we couldn't have children. They did tell him he had a low sperm count. He'd dabbled his share with drugs in the sixties; he wore Jockey shorts (you're supposed to wear boxers). He loved Jacuzzis; you're not supposed to take Jacuzzis. It's so ironic. To have grown up in the era we did, to have worried sick about birth control our whole lives, and then want to get pregnant and can't. It's just the original *"Ha!"*

I had two surgeries. I had my tubes blown out; I had dye tracing. Plus it puts a terrible strain on your sex life. I mean, we were a couple with a mission, there. When I got married, I only had about seventeen minutes of childbearing time left. They tell you the older you get, the fewer eggs you have. Well, I had one old egg on a walker. And everybody had a million ideas: "Stand on your head." "Put corn under the bed." "There's a castle in Ireland where you drink the water." And there's some restaurant in L.A. where if you eat the salad you get pregnant.

I'm amazed people work at getting pregnant for ten and fifteen years. I don't know how they stay married. The stress it puts on you— every time you get your period, it's like the death of a child. Now it's egg donors; that's the big thing in L.A. right now, interviewing egg donors. And birth mothers. As if there was any guarantee that because you pick a blond, blue-eyed Rhodes scholar, your kid is going to be brilliant and gorgeous! And not a serial killer.

After months and months of this ordeal, we made reservations to go to Mexico. Our vacation budget lessened as the years went by, but we were still doing pretty well, and Ixtapa was a wonderful resort. Somewhere along the way, we both looked at each other and realized the same thing: "We want to be parents more than we want to have a baby." Dennis said, "Okay, we're going on our vacation, and when we get back, let's talk to somebody about adoption."

Wow!

don't look back, we're not going that way

The most complicated
relationship of my life.

Oh, god,
what have we done?

I'm looking a little nervous here.

A girl and her best friend, Janie.

Sherry and me outside GI barracks where we lived.

I'm 5'9"
(with hair, 6'2").
The Fourth Wall
Players are
(from left to right)
Kent Broadhurst,
Bette-Jane Raphael,
Jeremy Stevens,
James Manis and
Marcia Wallace.

The best job in the world. Bill Daily, Bob Newhart, Marcia Wallace,
Suzanne Pleshette and Peter Bonerz (pictured left to right).

The biggest part I ever had on a TV show — *Magnum PI,*
with its stars, Tom Selleck and John Hillerman.

Jack Riley, me, Peter Bonerz, Suzie, and Bob
at one of our many reunion lunches.

I can't believe Denny saw me in this outfit and still asked me out: Tessie Tura in "Gypsy".

Edna and Principal Skinner caught *en flagrante* by Bart the demon.

Here's my *Simpsons* alter cartoon ego, Edna Krabappel. We are both chin-impaired, but she has longer lashes and I don't smoke. But then I haven't had Bart Simpson in the fourth grade for fifteen years, either.

MATT GROENING

I believe this picture speaks for itself.

My brother Jim in hog heaven with Suzanne Pleshette at my wedding.

Could we be any happier? I think not.

The Wallace girls: me, my sister Sherry and niece Kim.

Bob Newhart
bringing down the house
at my wedding.

Our "Please
Let Us Adopt
Your Child"
picture, 1988.

My beloved
Shalane,
who gave me
such a gift ...
my Mikey.

Jo Anne Worley and me in the female *Odd Couple*.
I'm messy, she's neat, just like real life.
Pictured left to right: Jackie Joseph, Eileen T'Kaye,
Patty Reagan, Jo Anne, me, and Julie Thornton.

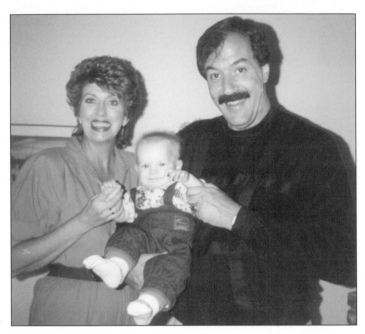

Our first Christmas.

The Judge, the lawyer (David Radis),
the parents and the boy on adoption day.

Poke and Joann,
almost fifty years later.

"Aaaaargh."
An L.A. pirate.

Brett Somers, Marcia Wallace:
a lifelong friendship.

THE PASADENA PLAYHOUSE

PRESENTS

A CELEBRATION
OF
LOVE AND FRIENDSHIP

FOR

MARCIA WALLACE
AND
DENNIS HAWLEY

MONDAY, JANUARY 13, 1992

8:00 P.M.

The program for
the Benefit.

Jo Anne Worley and Lily Tomlin with Denny and me at the Benefit.

We baked Daddy a cake on his birthday, even though he wasn't with us anymore.

Mikey with his
birth sister, Ashley.

Mikey in a cornfield.

My big old red head in the window of Saks for the "Fashion Against Breast Cancer" campaign, 1999.

That's My Bush. What a show. What a job. The genius of Matt Stone, Trey Parker, Kurt Fuller, Kristen Miller, Timothy Bottoms, John D'Aquino, Carrie Quinn Dolin, and me.

The picture I
treasure most.

A boy and
his proud mom
on graduation day
from middle school.

Farewell to Poke

But before we could start that journey, my daddy died, which was hard, but I was so happy there was nothing unresolved, unexpressed or unforgiven in our relationship. I had no regrets and a real sense of appreciation that he was my father. In a world of imitation, he was the real McCoy, a truly hilarious man whose dreams eluded him. Sales was his life. (He sold my car once when I was sleeping; he also sold our garage and the dog.) And like many the American, he figured if you're on the teevee, you're rich (damn those *Friends* actors). So he always thought I was holding out on him. He once followed me into a closet, shut the door, and as we stood there in the dark, nose to nose, with a coat sleeve flapping in my face, I heard him say, "Just buy me one Holiday Inn. Just one Holiday Inn." Well, Wallace Sundries is no more. But I'm sure he's somewhere selling my old gym socks and asking everybody if they ever saw *The Bob Newhart Show*.

And it's so ironic. He overcame throat cancer, lung cancer, open-heart surgery, and none of those killed him. He just ... died. I guess he'd done enough. I miss him to this very day.

So First You Place an Ad in the Paper

After the funeral, I made an appointment with a woman, now a good friend of mine, Beverly Sanders, and her husband, Harvey Newmark, and they taught us many things about what not to do in terms of adoption. They had a heartbreaking experience; they had adopted a daughter, Leah, and after three months, the mother came and took her back. Which is awful. So we saw a lot of Beverly and Harvey, and they turned us on to this attorney by the name of David Radis. So we went to see David. And he said on the phone, "Okay, here's how it goes. I do private adoptions, and over the years, I have met a lot of birth mothers or know people who know birth mothers. I also urge you to advertise."

Now this is done all the time, but back then advertising for a baby was pretty unusual, and our friends were very nervous: "What are you going to do? You're on television. They know you; they'll blackmail you. What are you going to do?"

But I didn't want to get on a plane and bring back a stranger. We both wanted to be part of the gestational period. And neither one of us were afraid; we knew we weren't going to be blackmailed. And if anything felt wrong, we would walk. That was certainly one of the things I attribute to Buddhism: knowing that my baby would find me.

Denny was so organized; he got the folders, and he got all the information. By now he had left the Breakers and was starting to renovate a residential hotel called the Chancellor in downtown L.A. A short-term job, something he could do in his sleep. So he just really got into this adoption process. And of course I did, too.

They gave us a list of papers to advertise in. They said forget the newspapers in big cities, because the girls are more savvy there and they tend to want more money and everything. So I just put it out there. I mean, I called everybody I knew. I called everybody I went to college with. It was right up my alley; I was a woman with another mission. I called every doctor I knew, every lawyer I knew, everybody—I told the box boy at the supermarket I was looking for a birth mother. And when I look back on it now, I think people must have thought I was certifiable. "Hello. Nice to meet you. Do you know any potential birth mothers? Have a nice day."

When we went to see David, he said to advertise in Shreveport and Lincoln, Nebraska, and towns like that. So we wrote the letter; it was like an audition letter. "Dear Birth Mother: We are so in love, and we are not too fat and not too thin and not too poor..." And David, whom we adored, said, "Now, don't be telling them you're no Buddhist. Those girls will think their baby's not going to have Christmas." I said, "Okay, I'll keep my mouth shut." (As you know by now, not my natural bent.)

Then Jo Anne and I went to Traverse City, Michigan, to do the female *Odd Couple*. After that, Denny and I went to help my mother move out of her house into an apartment after my dad's death. We got a call from David, "Quick, send a picture to Mindy in Butte who's looking for adoptive parents." There we were desperately running around Creston, Iowa, trying to find somebody with a camera to take a picture of us looking not too ugly, not too fat, not too old, not too demented (not so easy), and of course madly in love (easy). My friends Linda and Jim Hartsock came to the camera rescue. To audition for some fifteen-year-old girl who lives in Montana. I've still got the picture in the kitchen; I've got my arms around Denny. It was so cool, because he's in his shorts and we're on the front steps of the house I grew up in.

So we get the picture, and we had already written the letter. Once we put it out there in the universe, of course, we had babies falling out of the sky.

I was on the road again with *The Odd Couple* when David called and said, "Well, this adoptive couple got divorced and this baby is available. It's being born Tuesday, and they picked you."

I called Denny: *"We've got a baby! We've got a baby! We've got to get the baby right away! WE'VE GOT TO GET THE BABY!"*

He said, "Marcia, you're on the road. I'm here working. What am I going to do? Leave the baby home alone to watch TV during the day? Settle down. There'll be another baby."

Twenty minutes later, my friend Sally Marshall called and said, "I have this baby, but it's six months old and has been living with its mother." Well, I had learned enough about adoption to know, and that's what you need a lawyer for, because he had told us, "Look, I've never had a birth mother change her mind. At least not after. I've had them change their minds before. But if her parents are hesitant, if anybody in the family is hesitant, if the birth father is hesitant—walk. Because there'll be other babies, and you don't want to have happen to you what happened to Beverly."

I didn't think we wanted a baby who'd been living with his

mother for six months. Besides, we wanted a newborn. I wanted to make my own mistakes. I didn't care what race it was. Denny said, "Call me crazy, but I don't mind saying I want a white baby. I want the baby to look like it could be ours." (And that all worked out for the best, really.) We also we wanted to be part of the pregnancy time.

Next, You Go Out on Interviews

Then David called and said, "I have a birth mother. What happened, the adoptive mother changed her mind, and so the birth mother wants to place her baby with someone else. What I do is usually give her the names of five couples, and she interviews them."

We were going to be interviewed!

Well, she called me first—Shalane Moras—and she never called anyone else.

As it turned out, the first adoptive mother was a Hollywood actress. She had answered Shalane's ad; she was on a second marriage and wanted a baby. But then her sister-in-law got pregnant, and the actress decided she wanted to have a baby first. That meant Shalane was available again. She called me, and and the rest is adoption history (and another wacky Hollywood story). I always knew my baby would find me.

Anyway, I was in New York doing a commercial in September of 1987 and I said, "Look, let me fly back through Shreveport" (which is where Shalane was), "and we'll meet." I wish I could remember the name of the hotel. Not the Dew Drop Inn, but something like that. So there I am in this awful motel in Shreveport, Louisiana, and this darling girl walks in.

"Well," she says in her cute accent, "Ah wahnted to tell you in person, Ah am a recovering alcoholic."

"It's okay," I say, "I'm a Buddhist."

And we both laughed.

I always said, if I had given birth, the baby would be from a fam-

ily of alcoholics with allergies. Mikey's birth family is a family of alcoholics with allergies. So I just loved Shalane, and I said, "Let's call
Denny." So we called Denny, and he talked to her, and we were just in
heaven. We signed the papers, and she told us the baby was going to
be born in January.

Now, of all the things that I have done in my life—I mean,
meeting Denny was incredible—but of all the things I've ever done
in my life that could be termed magic, this adoption was it. It just
seemed that nothing could go wrong. It was perfect from the beginning to the end, the way we found her and the way we chose each
other.

We decided to bring her out a couple of months before the
birth, because we really wanted to get to know her. I had read that
fetuses could hear in the womb, and I never wanted to get on a plane
and bring home a strange baby. So Shalane came out to L.A. We didn't
want her living with us—we thought that was a bit much—but there
was a very sweet woman who ran a home for birth mothers, so
Shalane lived there, and we saw her all the time. And every time we
met somebody, I would say, "This is our birth mother, Shalane," and
eyes would roll in the back of the heads, and you'd see them sort of
inching away: "Well, isn't that special?" á la the Church Lady. But we
just couldn't care less.

And of course every time I took her to the doctor, they thought
I was the grandmother. But that's all right. After all, she was twenty
years younger than me, and I was forty-four years old. But we adored
her and she adored us, and she spent Thanksgiving and Christmas
with us. It seemed a strange setup to my mother, but she did her best
to keep up. My sister was great; she did a lot with and for Shalane and
made her feel very much at home.

We used to chant together, Shalane and I, and I used to talk to
her stomach. She was in many ways a daughter to me; we were very,
very, very close. And she was funny, and stubborn, and tenacious, and
troubled, and smart, and darling, and angry, and any number of

things, not unlike my own self.

She'd met the birth father in rehab. She had had a substance abuse problem for quite some time, and gone into rehab, and met this guy, Greg, and gotten pregnant. What happened with her happened with a lot of women. Denny and I went to this workshop for adoption. The first person I heard speak was a woman called Sharon; she had three of her own kids besides the ones she adopted. She called them "homemade" and "adopted." She said, "Here's what people think about adoptive parents: they're saints. Here's what people think about birth mothers: they're trailer trash. But it's never that simple."

It's usually a young girl, younger than Shalane—Shalane was twenty-five. She had already had one child, and that was important to me. She had raised her until she was three, and she knew how hard it was, so she had no romantic vision. People said, "You're on television; she's going to come back to your door." And I said, "So what? I'll always be happy to see her." Our feeling was always that we're his parents, and you can't have too many people who love you. And the truth never hurt anybody. Maybe this comes from having had a rocky relationship with my own parents, but I knew that birthing has nothing to do with parenting.

She had hoped to marry the birth father, and then he changed his mind and wanted her to have an abortion. And in her defense she said, "No, I'm going to have this child." So that when Mikey asked me the question you're not supposed to ask till you're a teenager, "Why did she give me away?" I said, "Well, just because you can have a baby doesn't mean you're ready to be a parent, and isn't it great? She said, 'I'm going to find the perfect mom and dad for my boy,' and she picked Daddy and me. Isn't that great?"

Shalane and Denny and I spent an enormous amount of time together, and it was just a magical time for all of us. And even though it made some people a little nervous, we never even noticed, because we were so happy.

And Then You've Got the Job: Parent!

I had wanted a girl so bad I used to chant, "Please, I want a girl. Please let it be a girl." But it was my good fortune to find out his sex almost at the beginning, or the beginning of when Shalane came out here. I remember Denny waited outside in the doctor's waiting room, and I took Shalane in and we saw the sonogram. I remember the doctor saying, "God, I hope this baby slows down when he gets out." Shalane always said he danced on her bladder. But you could see the penis, because he was still breach; he hadn't turned. And I remember thinking, "Ohhhhh..."

But I was so glad later that I knew then, so that there wouldn't be a moment in the delivery room where anybody would feel my disappointment in any way. Now, I couldn't be more thrilled. But I went out and said to Denny, "It's a boy," and I saw how excited he was. We had already decided on names: Michael Wallace Hawley if it was a boy, and Annie Wallace Hawley if it was a girl.

We had a wonderful Christmas all together. I remember dragging Shalane all over town: "This is our birth mother! This is our birth mother!" And I remember the day Denny and I walked down to BabyLand and got the crib. Oh, it was an unbearably glorious, happy time! Once again I had more showers than you could shake a stick at, baby ones this time. And Shalane moved in with us two weeks before the birth.

On January 28, 1988, I took Shalane to lunch at Paramount, and she saw Michael J. Fox. Now, supposedly Michael J. Fox looks a lot like Mikey's birth father. And whenever Shalane got excited, she'd go, "Oh-oh-sha! Oh!" It's some Louisiana thing, and she'd shake her wrists. Well, she saw Michael J. Fox and went right into labor!

But we went home to wait. And around one-thirty in the morning she came into our room and said, "Y'all, it's time." And I was like Lucy, like Ricky actually—I was like Ricky Ricardo! Because I slept with no clothes on in those days, and I got up and I just twirled! "Oh!

Oh! Where's my, where's my—!" Dennis had to take me by the shoulders and dress me, because I was just beside myself.

So we drove her there—Tarzana Hospital—and the obstetrician, Dr. Fred Powell, was an adoptive father. He'd done a lot of this kind of thing, so he wasn't shocked to see me and Denny there. And poor Shalane, she was yelling, "Drugs! Give me drugs!" But it was too late; they wouldn't because she had this fever. We thought maybe there was some sort of protection in that; she had this phantom high fever for no reason, and it went away just after he was born. Maybe she wasn't supposed to have an epidural.

So she had natural childbirth. She'd had some Lamaze training. We were her coaches. She hadn't wanted to go to a Lamaze class, so we'd arranged for a Lamaze teacher come to her. She hated this woman, and she bristled at being told what to do, just like we did. So we just sort of backed off. But we got the breathing down; we were doing the breathing. So she had natural childbirth. Not that she wanted to, but she had it.

She was making a lot of noise, but not screaming. I remember we both rubbed her. She wanted to be rubbed, and then she didn't want to be touched, then she wanted to be rubbed. We rubbed her legs, and I kept thinking, "I don't suppose I could take a break; I guess I should keep going. She's doing the birthing, but I'm *so* tired!" Afterwards, I thought, "Adoptive mothers all say, 'Oh, if only I could have given birth.'" Not me. This was fine by me! Giving birth looks hard, and it looks like it really hurts. Hurts like hell. And I mean, how could I? I couldn't have done better. First of all, Shalane took far better care of herself than I ever would have done, with her vegetables and her milk. Oh! She just took such good care of herself.

Anyway, she was in labor from one a.m. until he was born at 9:12 a.m. We felt... it was like he came from all three of us. We all breathed in unison, we all pushed in unison, and it was like this baby came out from all three of us. And everybody burst into tears. The nurse, the doctor, us—we all burst into tears. And Mikey, too. It was unbelievable. It was scary. Oh, god, is he going to be okay? And then the doctor was so great: "Well, the cord's around his neck," and he just sort of twisted him like a corkscrew. And she's so tiny, Shalane—how do they do that, turn a baby around? But they did, and there he was. Denny cut the cord, they gave the baby to me, I tripped, and they took him away. Dennis stayed with Shalane; he was so sweet. And she said, "Go be with your son."

They gave us a room with the baby, and they took Shalane off to the surgical floor. She chose not to see him. She said, "I don't wanna bond with him, 'cause I bonded with Ashley, and I don't want to bond; I know it'll make you feel bad. So I don't want to bond."

She didn't want to hold him or see him. She still had the fever, so they took her up to the medical floor. But, hon, five days later, she was feeling terrific, with the flat stomach and the high heels.

And there we were on the maternity floor, taking a thousand pictures. And Sherry came from work, and, of course, took her position as the Aunt of the Century. We stayed there with Mikey all day, and that was when Barbara Powell, the wife of the obstetrician, came to see us and gave us a wonderful gift. A framed poem:

> Neither flesh of my flesh nor bone of my bone,
> But miraculously my own.
> Never forget for a single minute
> You didn't grow under my heart, but in it.

And after that we went home and fell into our bed.

Yes, Sir, That's My Baby

Mikey didn't come with us; this was 1988, and in those days they didn't send babies home right away. There was nothing wrong with him; they just kept him for eighteen hours. Somebody had come into the room and said, "Nine on the APGAR." I said, "Fine by me, I don't have a clue what you're talking about." It's starting already, huh?

The next morning we woke up; we were so excited. And we brought the baby seat, and went to the hospital and got him. They put me in a wheelchair like I was a real mother! And they wheeled us out—after all that tripping I did, they were probably very right—and we brought him home.

We were just beside ourselves. I remember we were up all that night. When I came down the next morning, there was Dennis, lying on the couch with no clothes on, and the baby (also with no clothes on) lying on his chest, both sound asleep.

And Dennis—nobody loved his sleep more than Dennis—he used to say, "Do you want Daddy to rock you?" For years and years he would sit up in the rocking chair and rock his boy.

March 1, 1988

Dearest Wendy,

    It's happened; I'm a mother. The Boy was born on January 29, 1988. He weighed seven pounds and his name is Michael Wallace Hawley. He arrived with a seeking spirit, a fondness for raisin commercials and hair that sticks straight up. Of course I did gain that pesky twenty-five pounds, no small feat since he was adopted. Actually I gained two more pounds than the birth mother.

    Of course we are a little long in the tooth to be first time parents. We're the only people at Toys R Us with reading glasses. (I can't even fake it anymore. If I show up at a restaurant without my glasses, I have to ask the people in the next booth to hold my menu for me.) Last week I was at a swank cocktail party, all dressed up, sipping champagne, munching canapés, and I suddenly realized I was rocking back and forth humming "Wake Up, Toes" (Mikey's personal favorite). But I figure there's a plus to becoming a parent in my middle years; by the time he turns on me, I'll be deaf and won't hear him.

    Careerwise, the hubby is general manager of a new boutique hotel in West Hollywood, The Valadon. Boy, am I a lucky woman: all this and room service, too. As for me, I do some plays and commercials and of course my art film career is moving right along (Dame Judi Dench is very nervous). Featured roles in Teen Witch, My Mother the Werewolf, *and (dare I get my hopes up?) possibly a part in* Space Sluts in the Slammer.

I hope your life is as great as mine, dear friend.

Love,

Marcia

12 don't look back →

Mad About the Boy

I'm so grateful none of our trying to get me pregnant worked, because I can't imagine having a child other than Mikey. He's the world's greatest kid.

Bringing the baby home for the first time, that really turns your life upside down. Nobody can tell you how great it is, and nobody can tell you how hard it is. *Nobody*. Dennis and I never had a fight until we became parents. Because you're so totally sleep-deprived. Mikey was a very good baby until he was around nine months, and then he started waking up all night long. After that we started letting him fall asleep wherever he wanted to. Boy, if I had it to do over again, that kid would have been in his bed from the beginning. But ... *don't look back*!

My mother saw Mikey for the first time when he was six months old and she came out with my brother Jim, his wife Beth, and their six-month-old daughter Kathleen to celebrate the formalizing of the adoption. Each state has their adoption laws, and in California, there's a six-month waiting period before it's final.

We rented a limo from our friend Hubie Banks of Unicorn Limo, and Dennis's former boss brought his video camera to record the occasion. But when the camera was on, he thought it was off, and when it was off he thought it was on, so he didn't get any of the ceremony. All he had were pictures of feet as he was swinging it in his hand. Just pictures of feet and the floor. Denny told me, "We can't say anything to him, he'll feel so bad." I said, *"But we didn't get any of the ceremony! We didn't get ANY!"*

This adoption ceremony was a big thing. Shalane had signed the papers when Mikey was born, but any time in the next six months, she could have changed her mind and seen a lawyer and taken it to court and gotten Mikey back.

We tried to find the biological father, too. We didn't succeed, but if you can show proof of having tried to find him, then he has no claim. But the fact is, he didn't want this baby. Shalane was always trying to get me a picture of him to show to Mikey, but he never even could get it together to send her one.

There's No Stork, Kid—You Were Brought
By a Lawyer

From the time Mikey was born, we always said, "We're so glad we adopted you." And we decided we would always tell him the truth. When he asked, "Did I grow in your tummy?" I'd say, "No, you grew in another lady's tummy and came home with us. Kids come to families in different ways. Some grow in their mom's tummies and come home, and some grow in another lady's tummy." And he always said, "Okay, fine."

When Mikey was a year and a half, the lawyer called. Another child was available for adoption, and were we interested? I thought for sure Dennis was going to say yes. But he said no, and he wouldn't budge. I was so shocked. That was our first real rift. We went to counseling about it, and we were sitting there with this guy, and it was the first time I'd ever seen Dennis cry. He was crying, and he said, "I'm so afraid she'll never forgive me, but I have such a bad feeling about this. I can't do it." He was never able to explain it. He obviously had a terrible feeling of dread.

But nobody enjoyed their kid more than Dennis did, spent more time with him, with more patience. I'd come down in the morning and already he'd be there with the camcorder, filming away. Looking back now, I think I know why Mikey is so interesting. Dennis would do whole plays and put them on tape, about Elmer the Worm, and Mikey was the star. He's got the worm, and squash all over his face, and he's got hats on, and a costume, and of course the kid's only six months old. But he had all this stimulation.

I'd get up with him one day of the weekend, and Denny would get up on the other. Usually it's mothers who are more protective, but I was always throwing that poor kid over my shoulder, going out in the rain early in the morning. Sometimes, Dennis would run out after me through the bushes with his hair askew, in his underwear: "Give me that baby! Get that baby out of this! The rain and the elements! What's the matter with you?"

Denny was always very cautious with him. In the pictures Mikey drew of his dad later, the body language is unbelievable: wide-open arms, big smile, moustache. I'm sure everybody thinks this is an exaggeration, but I never knew a better parent.

When Mikey was in nursery school at Play Mountain Place, I'd come to pick them up, and Denny would have six kids on his lap. He said more than once, "I wasn't ready to meet you and love you earlier, but I wish I was, because then we could have had a big family."

But there're all kinds of families in the new millennium. And in our family, the birth mother comes for Easter dinner. That's how it goes.

About six years later, Shalane became pregnant again, and made the choice to make another childless couple extremely happy. I didn't tell many people about this baby because people can be judgmental. Someone I did tell said to me, "What's the matter? Can't she keep her legs together?" (How picturesque.) Listen, Shalane is a wonderful girl, smart, loving, generous of spirit. She gave me the greatest gift of my life, and I am very protective of her. Anyway, she came to L.A. to have the baby. After Carly was born, I asked Shalane if she wanted to meet Mikey. And she said, "Well..." And I said, "Mikey, do you want to meet

Shalane?" Because I had always told him about her, and answered all of his questions. ("Yes, but who's my real mom?" "Me." "But who's my *real* mom?" "Mikey, your real mom is the one who keeps you safe, and reads to you, and makes sure you're warm and fed and happy—that's your real mom. I'm your real mom.")

So I said to Mikey, "Do you want to meet Shalane?" And he said yes. I wouldn't have sought this out, except she was in L.A., and you never know when the chance will come again. I thought this could be very important for both of them. I mean, life is short and precious. She was supposed to spend the night with us, and she called and cancelled. Mikey said, "Well, sure, I got a stomach ache for nothing."

But I went to get her the next morning, and she came over, and they sort of shook hands. She said, "Michael, do you have any questions for me?" And he said, "Yes. What did I feel like in your tummy?" And she took his hand, and she tickled the palm. Which was so great. And he said, "Okay, fine." And he never asked anything else.

Clearly, she wasn't trying to "win" Mikey's affections away from me. I watched the two of them play, and they look exactly alike. It made me so happy, and I thought, "God, I'm weird. It made me happy."

Shalane's first daughter, Ashley, is five years older than Mikey. I always urged Shalane to tell Ashley about Mikey, because too many people knew. At the adoption seminar we'd gone to, the woman who ran it gave us all this great advice. She said, "Always let them know they're adopted, and always answer their questions, but information about other siblings? Wait till they're about seven." So I did, and when he asked me if he had any, I said, "Yes, a sister."

So Ashley and Mikey started talking on the phone. And then we flew Ashley out and she spent a week with us. It was amazing: she tortured him, ignored him, played with him, hugged him, just like a normal teenage big sister. And he, of course, adored her and followed her around like any little brother would do.

I thought it went very well. I did my part. I didn't want there to be any gaps. I didn't want him to have to be on the Internet someday trying to track down his birth family. I felt this was my gift to him. I'll always be his mother, but I understand how it must feel; I'd want to know, too. To be able to look into the face of your sibling and say, "Oh, there's my nose; there's my eyes."

The lawyer told us we were the exception. Most people are just not that comfortable. He said he never saw this relationship work as well with anybody as it did with us and Shalane. We wanted adoption to be an issue, not *the issue*, of Mikey's life. The usual protocol was not telling the kid at all, which is so mean and cruel. Or sitting him down around twelve, when he's going through puberty: *"Oh, and by the way, we're not your real parents."*

Growing up, I always thought *I* was adopted. I look like a carbon copy of my mother, but still, I always imagined I had other parents. I think a lot of kids do, or *wish* they were. Somebody once said to me, "Mikey was abandoned twice; once by his birth mother, and once by his father." Well, maybe that's true; I don't know. But we have an awfully strong tie, Shalane and I. And I will treasure and love her till the day I die. I mean, look at the gift she gave me!

I guess the reason a lot of adoptive parents don't want their kids to know the birth mother is fear; they're afraid they'll go off with her instead. But kids growing up in households always pick up on fear. Always. They may not understand what the deal is, but they always know. I guess it's a fear that "blood will out." Never mind that this is a relationship that has been developed over years, a relationship that has developed over a child's whole lifetime. The mythology is that just because a person comes along and says, "You're my blood," the kid is going to say, "Wow, that's the real deal. Let's go." I don't think that happens. Ever. I'm told that very few boys want to do anything towards knowing their birth mother. But putting myself in Mikey's place, I would want to know everything. I couldn't imagine not knowing.

And as I said, the more people who love you, the better.

December 20, 1990

Dearest Wendy,

   Happy holidays. I hope everyone is well, but, hon, what happened to the eighties? They're gone, they're history, they're a Trivial Pursuit game already. Doesn't it seem just like yesterday that we were tooling around Fairfield in Alphonse the Peugeot? (You don't still have him, do you?) It's going by a little tooo fast for my speed.

   I really liked the eighties. I finally turned forty and caught up with my face. But, oh, what a shock, I went blithely to my mailbox one day and found an invitation to my thirtieth high school reunion. Are you going to yours? And guess what? I went, I had a great time, and I thought we all looked great; very lifelike. And trust me, I was the only one there with a toddler.

   Speaking of which, I have a few things to tell you about The Boy. (Hey, it's my job, and you know all this, but humor me.) Dennis and I love being parents. Mikey Hawley is almost three (he's the short one in the picture). There's just no preparing anyone for this incredible adventure of parenthood. I had no idea how hard it would be, and I had no idea how wonderful it would be. People try and tell you, but go know, until you're finally a mom and dad...

   And then, just when you think you're on top of it, they switch their modus operandi. I was thinking the other day that the twos weren't so terrible, and that very next morning he woke up and said to himself, "Whoa, I've been two for ten months now and I haven't caused nearly enough trouble; I'm way behind. I've got tantrums to throw. I've got a reputation to uphold. I better increase my daily quota of 'No's to about six hundred before lunch." It's like his favorite movie stopped being "The Little Mermaid" and became "The Omen."

   And your basic toilet training is going rather slowly. However, in spite of this occasional appearance as the Terminator, Mikey Hawley is still the world's most irresistible child. He's funny and smart and loving and curious. Ah, yes, curious. Before he was born, I used to lie on my couch with the remote control and say to Dennis, "Oh, honey, I hope we have a curious child."

Oooops, be careful what you wish for—he flushed the remote control down the toilet, and I haven't been on that couch in almost three years. Now here we are, Dennis and I, out in that back yard throwing that ball 786 times a day; this from a woman who flunked gym and once made a vow, á la Scarlett O'Hara, never to run again. That's how much I love this boy, this miracle boy.

I just appreciate my life so much, my family and friends and work.

Of course, you do have to work harder at romance with a child in your lives. Less time to play the Shepherd and the Pizza Waitress. We'd love to get away more, but raising a child has cut into our vacation budget. Five years ago we went to Europe, four years ago Bora Bora, three years ago Mexico, two years ago Palm Springs, one year ago Las Vegas and this year Sacramento.

We'd already started saving for next year's trip to Fresno when we had an opportunity to go on a Caribbean cruise. We were so thrilled, but we won the Dramamine Award for the trip. I was asked to participate in "A Salute to Comedy" on board. Well, hon, I could barely stand, let alone salute. Of course that didn't stop me from gaining about a pound an hour. It's the worst feeling, because you're not only sick, you're trapped and everybody has a remedy, and I was willing to try them all: lying down, standing up, eating crackers standing on your head, going on deck, going to bed, having sex with the captain. I heard them all. I guess I'm just not a cruising kind of gal.

I was so happy to see terra firma again, my beautiful new house (oh, yes, after seventeen years up on Appian Way, we sold the house and moved to a house with more room and a yard), my beautiful boy, my beautiful dog. Oh, yes, we have a puppy, my first puppy. Bingo is his name and he's a Vizsla, a Hungarian hunting dog.

Well, since we don't have an abundance of quail and pheasant in our back yard, he's taken to hunting underwear. Seems kind of kinky to me, but who am I to judge? I love my dog. We got Bingo after our dog Dr. Pepper bought the farm. The Doc was never a happy dog; we were his fourth owners, and his dreams eluded him. I thought of trying to find him another home, but had trouble with the ad: "Thirteen-year-old cranky poodle, doesn't like any other living thing, open sores, needs loving home."

Anyway, I did my best and held his head at the end and told him, "Don't be scared; when you wake up, you'll be a puppy again." Our karma together wasn't yet finished, however. I had him cremated, and usually the ashes come back in a tasteful pine box. Pepper's came back in a fruitcake tin. Next, I decided to scatter his ashes at the beach, since he actually had a good time there for about twenty minutes once, but when I tried they blew back in my face.

Dennis is still the classiest hotel man in town, and I've had some interesting roles this year, including Olive in another production of the female The Odd Couple; *a sex-starved spinster strangled with her own tongue in* Ghoulies Go To College *(I'm sure Meryl Streep was sick about missing that one); and Mrs. Krabappel, Bart's teacher in* The Simpsons, *which I've absolutely loved doing. It's so great to get paid for doing what you love to do. I've been so fortunate.*

Love,

Marcia & Dennis

13 don't look back

It Can't Happen to Us ...

Christmas 1992

Hi Everybody,

Every two years since 1980 I have sent out a Christmas letter. It's become kind of a tradition and I enjoy doing it, since I love Christmas and I love my friends. This is the year for the letter, but something terrible happened in 1992 that, for a long time, I didn't think there was any way I could do the letter. Now, I think there's no way I could not do it...

After Dennis finished his job renovating the Chancellor Hotel, he decided he wanted to stay home for a while just to be with Mikey. This lasted for a blissful six months, until I got a job on the road and took Mikey along.

Now, let me say again that I get terrible reviews. So when someone called and said "We're doing a production of *You're a Good Man, Charlie Brown* with Billy Barnes and Jo Anne Worley, and it's in San Francisco and Sacramento and Santa Barbara, and we want you to play Peppermint Patty," I read it, and I thought, "There's no part, there's no jokes and there's no songs, so at least I can't get bad reviews. What are the chances? Nothing to do; no one's going to notice me." And the reviews said, "Near-perfect cast. Except for—" guess who?

We were in rehearsal when Mikey first rolled over. We all stopped the show and applauded him and raved and screamed and yelled. I think that's why he loves applause so much now. The show was kind of a geriatric version of *Peanuts*, and we played in a huge theater, the Geary—way too big for this particular thing. But throughout the show Mikey would sit happily backstage in his little bouncer, with his "nanny" looking after him—Nanny Zack, we called him. Zack was an old friend, and he was great. He used to take Mikey to the Castro district and carry him around in his backpack, because it just made him feel so butch. He was great fun. I'm sad to say Zack has since died of AIDS.

Denny would send us notes: "Marcia and Mikey, I love you and I miss you like crazy." And then he would come up on the weekends, until he got a new job at the Valadon.

This was a charming little hotel just off the Sunset Strip. Mikey and I would come down when he'd be on as the weekend manager, and we'd spend the weekend with him. And we always had great fun! A charming, charming place.

That was Mikey's first year. So for the first six months of Mikey's life, he had both his parents home. And his Aunt Sherry, with whom he has had an ongoing love affair. But I took him just about everywhere; that was my natural bent.

Then Denny left the Valadon and went to the Brentwood Suites, again to renovate. Dennis could have any number of high-paying fabulous jobs in another city, but as his mother used to say, he lost his ambition. And that was true, in a way, because he was so thrilled just being a husband and father. And I couldn't move somewhere else and still work in show biz.

When we met, he had a steady job and he paid the "rent," and whenever I worked, it was for the perks. Then things started to get tough for me. Well, there was a writers' strike and nobody was working; and right before the strike, I thought I had a part in a series, and then it was cancelled. I had a couple of things fall through bigtime. But I was just so darned happy otherwise.

I remember once I was in a kind of group therapy session, and someone said, "Look, it seems to me that you think you don't deserve both work and love." I pooh-poohed that, and I laughed in his face, but the point is, once I found love, my "money karma" and "work karma" pretty much *did* go to hell. Still, I don't know if that's true, on some deep and desperately fundamental level, or it was just coincidence. I don't know.

Money Can't Buy You Love, But It Helps Pay the Rent

At the same time Dennis started saying, "Look, we need our own house." That was okay with me, really. Although my house on the hill was very good to me; I had owned it for almost twenty years. I had equity in my house. I could refinance my house when I needed cash; it was a great investment. And I bought it when no one was buying houses. And you know, it's not that he didn't like it. It was a fun house, it was a great house, and I loved that house; we brought Mikey home there. But Denny wanted *our* house.

It was partly because my house wasn't at all a kid's house. I mean, it was two stories, with these steep steps with the open slats; we had to have everything barricaded at the bottom. One day I couldn't find Mikey. He had broken through the barricade, crawled up the stairs, out the doggy door, and gone out onto the roof! I burst out; he was turning around and going, "Aye-aye-aye!" And I screamed, *"Mikey!!"* And I thought, "I'll never get to him before he falls off the edge," but somehow I did. But I thought then, "Oh, god, this is not a kid's house."

So we started house-hunting. I guess we were in kind of denial, because we started looking at a time that was a seller's market, but we found this house and we were thrilled beyond belief. We didn't even make it past the living room before we looked at each other and said, "This is it." And we made a bid; we bid the asking price. Those were the days when people were bidding above. But it was our dream house. Plus, we sold the house up on the hill right away. It was in escrow, at least. We thought, "Hey, it's in escrow; what could happen?" So we got a swing loan to get in our house down on Genesee.

And then my next-door neighbor said she checked, and, "Oh, by the way, my property line goes three feet into your house." Now, this is not like waking up one day and finding out you now have a back-yard where you can keep horses. Three feet! What can you do with three feet? But she held up the escrow, the buyers dropped out, and we ended up having to support two houses for a year and a half.

So you watch your profits go, your savings go, and then you have to start borrowing money to keep both houses going. I try not to look back, in terms of regrets, because Denny was supposed to be in *our* house; he loved our house. Later, he said he wondered whether we should have stayed up on the hill. But eventually the house sold.

We moved into the new place when Mikey was a year and half. I have great videotapes of our first Christmas; my mother was with us, and Denny was cooking up a storm. We loved it; we were wildly happy here. He was still working at the Brentwood Suites. I wasn't working much at all. Somehow we kept scrambling to get by.

By this time we were in desperate debt. It doesn't take long to get behind in L.A. To add to everything, we had a tax problem. In the years I was earning plenty of money, my should-have-been-former business manager (who never left me in the dust) and beloved friend Howard Borris had set up a series of tax shelters. Tax shelters were all the rage.

Anyway, sure enough, one day I was up in the house on the hill and this guy I thought was selling brushes or something came to the door. He said, "Hello, I'm from the IRS, and you owe us $75,000, and I'm here for a check."

I said, "Excuse me, you want a check".

"Yes, I want a check. You can write me a check right now."

"And that would be for $75,000?"

"Yes."

I said, "You must pardon me; I'll be calling someone." So sure enough, these pesky tax shelters had been declared invalid. Now, I didn't even resent that, because I had use of that money all those years. The point is, it was declared invalid at the worst possible time. To pay it off, I had to dissolve my retirement fund. It had taken me twenty years to save $120,000, and about an hour and half to spend it.

So I paid the IRS the $75,000, but you know when you dissolve your retirement fund, you're penalized, so you owe them $35,000 on that, too. So that's when they slammed the a lien on the house. Now we couldn't get credit. And suddenly my "money karma" deserted me; it used to be that even when I only made thirty-five dollars a week, it was enough. I'd always made whatever I'd needed. And suddenly it was just gone. Everything was just awful. And nothing was enough.

I kept thinking, "Well, it can't get worse." And then it did get worse. We had had these glorious six years: incredible excitement, love, a family, baby, marriage, travel. Then, when it went to hell, it really went to hell.

Denny's Bad News

One day in January, Denny came home early. He had gone to work as usual, but he came home about ten. He said, "Well, that's it. The job's over. I've done my part." Meaning he'd done his part, and now they could get someone much cheaper to come in. I remember thinking, "Oh, we're so broke, and this is awful." But little did I know how much worse it was going to get.

The one good thing about that year was that I was working more, although I was on the road a lot. I did a couple of plays where Mikey had to stay home with Denny. It seemed awful at the time, but now in retrospect I think, "He had all that time with his boy." He said at the time, "I always thought anyone who's out of work should get out there and drive a cab. Now I'm there, and I don't want to drive a cab. I don't want to do anything like that."

He would tell me, "You're so understanding, you're so great, because I should be working," and I used to say, "Hey, you're doing all the cooking, all the cleaning, all the childcare, *and* you're looking for work." He sent out something like six hundred résumés during that year. He made calls, he just did everything he could, and took care of Mikey and took care of the house and everything. Still, he was always saying how grateful he was to me for not "hawking" him about it. But I reminded him, "Hey, I'm an actor, I'm out of work a lot." But he really appreciated that.

Now, as long as I was working, as long as one of us was working, he was fine. But if neither of us was working, he felt it was up to him. He should be making a living; he should be doing something. He got very depressed about that. But this was not a guy who sat in the corner and didn't do anything. He was always doing everything. Even though it seemed like a very rough year, and it was, as I look back on it now, we weren't really estranged. But if I had it to do over I'd have been a lot warmer to him.

I wasn't mad or anything like that; I was stressed. *Stressed.* I guess I shouldn't have minded—he didn't take drugs or hold up liquor stores—but he'd go to bed at 7:30. And that bothered me. I wish now I'd put my arms around him and kissed his back. But I would just turn over on my side and we'd be back-to-back in the bed. It was very stressful. There were tons of bills and we couldn't get credit.

But I never really nagged him. With all the mistakes I made, I never really said, "Get out there and get a job." I never did that. He was such a good guy and such a good husband.

So when the job ended and I went on the road, he was there with Mikey, and he carpooled and did everything. I was gone a lot that year. That was our main income.

And then I went to the Midwest to do *Steel Magnolias* with Dawn Wells. It was the fall of 1991. I remember my friend Angela Estell said she stopped in once while I was gone; she looked in the window and saw Denny just sitting there and she said he just looked so lonely. He came to the door, and he said, "I'll be so glad when Marcia gets home."

Anyway, while I was doing *Steel Magnolias* in Columbia,

Missouri, he called and said, "Guess what!" He'd gotten a job. He'd
gotten a job! A job in a hotel, not as general manager, but as person-
nel director, human resources. But he was so excited. And I came
home to do a reunion of *The Bob Newhart Show*.

Now Denny had always had, since I'd known him, a lot of stomach pain, and was always told it was an ulcer. Some times he'd be inca-
pacitated by it. But most of the time it was just something he dealt
with. But it had gotten worse and worse. In September 1991 we went
to the L.A. County Fair, and I remember he was in great pain, but I
had to go back on the road right after that.

We were gone for a long time, several weeks. I remember Mikey
would keep saying, "I want my daddy! I want my daddy!" He was
three and a half, but he was still using diapers. He was talking at a year
and half; he was traveling in planes. But he wanted to keep them diapers. He had his "poopy dance"; he'd get on his tiptoes and twirl, then
you'd have to put on the diapers and he'd poop in them. So, I thought,
"This trip is a great opportunity to get him off the diapers before he
goes from Pampers to Depends." But I remember thinking, "God, it's
stressful to be a kid," because it was like he was losing part of himself.
He was terrified. But he did it. We made it. But then it was, "I want
my daddy, want my daddy."

So Mikey and I came back. Denny had only been three weeks at
his new job, and he'd been having a lot of pain, so he drove to the doctor. He called me from there, and said, "Well, they think it's my gallbladder. They're going to remove it."

So they did. And I remember sitting in the waiting room with
this family of a woman who'd just found out she had breast cancer,
when the doctor came out and told me Denny's operation had turned
out fine. But Denny had never been in the hospital in his life, and the
nurses came out at one point and said, "Your husband needs to see
you." He had come out of the surgery so anxious, saying, "I want my
wife. I want my wife." So I went in there for a while and rubbed his
back, rubbed his feet. Looking back on it now, I think I felt uneasy
and unfinished, and was unnerved by that other family finding out

that their mother and wife had cancer.

Days after his surgery he was still in the hospital. They wouldn't let him go because he continued to run this high fever. But we thought, "That's just the aftereffects of the surgery; we're home free." Mikey and I would go visit him, and every time we left, Mikey would sob all the way home. He would sob, "I want my daddy, I want my daddy." Now he can hardly remember how much he loved his daddy. But there was a whole time when Denny was everything to him, mother *and* father. He would sob and sob, "I don't want my daddy to be in the hospital. I want my daddy." Then I had to go on the road again with Mikey.

The next time we came home, Mikey said, "Your eyes are yellow, Daddy."

Denny said to me, "Come with me into the kitchen. Look in my eyes. What do you see? Do my eyes look yellow?" And I said, "No, no, no."

And he said, "Oh, god, I just know I'm full of cancer. I just know. They're going to find out I'm full of cancer."

I was totally in denial. "Oh, don't be silly. I don't have any premonition." I thought, "I'm known for my premonitions; I'm known for my intuitions, my instincts. Everything's fine."

He went back to the doctor. Now, this was a doctor he had seen for many, many years, and he was crazy about Denny and me and everybody connected with us, and he was in denial, too. He said, "Oh, I'm sure it's just some sort of a gallstone from the surgery. From the gallbladder. I'm sure."

Then Denny called and said, "They're going to have do some sort of exploratory." Because his eyes were yellow, and there was obviously some bile or whatever, so they were going to have to do a laparoscopy. And when I called, he said, "Bad news. They think I might have pancreatic cancer."

And I screamed.

14 don't look back

→

... But It Did

Later there were some false negatives. But I think on some level, I knew. And then the horrible part of it is the insidiousness of this disease—it's so hard to find. He was down in Long Beach for tests, and I remember the first person I called of course was my sister Sherry, and I said, "They think Denny has pancreatic cancer." And Sherry, who has ESP about anything bad, she said she knew from the very first.

We both went down there, and the biopsy was negative and the MRI was negative; it was all negative. But there was this one guy who kept saying, "Look, I know what I saw. I saw a lesion on your pancreas." We, of course, wanted to believe the guy who said it was fine. That's what's so insidious—because the pancreas is behind the stomach, if you don't shoot it at the right angle, it can look like everything's fine. I remember sitting there with this guy who said, "Look, I'm sure it's a malignant lesion on your pancreas, and if it's operable, you've got about a thirty percent shot." And I said, "Well, fuck you and the horse you rode in on; this is not information I need."

We had an appointment with the surgeon after Thanksgiving. It was the worst Thanksgiving imaginable. We were supposed to go to Hugh and Ruth Maguire's, but then I think Denny's brother Doug came down, and we cooked a little turkey, and everybody was real busy not talking about what was going on. Then Mikey did something he had never done before. In the middle of the night, he woke up between us and projectile-vomited all over the room. Kind of a portent of things to come, wouldn't ya say?

The next day we went to the surgeon, and he said, "Look, we can't tell. We have to open you up and see what's doing. If it's operable, it might be malignant or it might be nothing. If it's operable, it'll be about an eleven-hour surgery."

We got up on Sunday and I drove him to UCLA. I didn't really know the medical center; I only knew where The Bin was. So I got lost, and Denny got this horrible diarrhea, and we couldn't find a bathroom, and we couldn't find the hospital. It was awful, just awful, and I thought, "My life is turning to shit here, literally." And so he got his room; I stayed there with him a long time, then I went home, and I came back early in the morning. He said, "Get in bed with me." So I stayed in bed with him and held him. And he went in to surgery.

We Have the Power

I had brought a whole bunch of inspirational stuff to read, anticipating this eleven-hour surgery, which is called a Whipple, where they remove part of your pancreas and just about everything else. They've come a long way, but we're still talking about the most deadly of all diseases. I remember my friends getting out their medical dictionary and looking it up, and we all wanted it to be like an infection, or this or that—anything but pancreatic cancer, which is about as deadly a malignancy as you can have.

My sister and I were there waiting—I didn't want anybody else with me—and this crazy guy comes through the lobby. And he's talking to himself; he was obviously on drugs. And he kept coming up to people and railing, just every bit of negativity, and I thought, "This is not a good sign; this is not a good sign."

And then about an hour and a half after the surgery started, I saw the doctor coming out, and he said, "I'm sorry, it's malignant. It's inoperable. I'm sorry."

We went back up to the room, and Denny came out of the anesthetic, and I said, "Well, it's bad news," and he said, "That's okay; we have the power."

I rubbed his legs and rubbed his feet, then started calling people to find him a good oncologist.

I called my oncologist, Dr. Jim Waisman, whom I adored, but he recommended a guy who was as nutty as a fruitcake. This was a guy who when he met you, when he came into the examining room to talk to you, he would start picking things off his chest and putting them in his mouth. Denny and I would look at each other, like, "Ewwww!" Then we found a radiologist, Dr. Robert Levy, because Denny had both chemo and radiology. The radiologist was a fabulous guy, someone who had almost died in an avalanche ten years earlier, so he was very spiritual, and really liked Dennis, and was really positive. But Denny never had a good day after that; he never had a well day.

I was in major denial, thinking, "How can I possibly make enough money to keep us in our house?" I mean, acting is a part-time job for Tom Cruise, but I wasn't working much, and of course Denny hadn't worked for a year, and we had tons of bills after the house debacle. We had a lot of perks in the hotel business, but insurance wasn't one of them. If it wasn't for my insurance he'd have died in some county hospital somewhere. So I thought, "I have to make enough money to keep my insurance going," so I was calling people, and my friends were calling people. And everybody said, "You're my hero and you're doing so great," but as I look back now, I was a lunatic. I was barely lucid, I was barely conscious, I was deranged beyond belief, and I was determined that he was going to make it.

The chemotherapy made Denny worse; the radiology made him worse. Brett came out to help drive him to his treatments, and lost him at the hospital. And of course did a lot of screaming and yelling:

"Got a fucking dying guy here, now move it! I mean it! Right now, or I'll have your head!" And she always said whenever she drove him, he'd try to get out and come around and try to open the door for her, and she said, "Dennis, I'm gonna have to smack you if you do that one more time."

He was a gentleman to the very end.

And then his mother came. And I had to be the one to tell her. Of course, I had told her that it was malignant, and then benign, and then malignant again; the whiplash from this, we all went through it. I never felt his mother was all that fond of me. In any case, we weren't close, but it didn't matter because Denny loved me, and we were the family. But now he just needed us all to get along. He wanted her there. And then she called his dad, Max. And they were a big help; they did lots of things. Max had to do *something*, even if it was to clean out the garage.

But I'd get up every morning and I'd go out in the kitchen and say, "Hello," and they'd just stare at the table. It was awful. It's not like in the movies where they say to Bette Davis, "You have six months to live," and she goes to Europe and looks great, then she gets a headache and lies down and dies. You always want to think it brings out the best in a family, and maybe it does in some. I know it must be agony losing your child, but Denny's mom, she wouldn't look at me or even acknowledge me. I'd say to her, *"Hey, I didn't give him cancer."*

I make it sound like I was this poor, sweet thing; I'm sure I had a part in this conflict, even if my memory of it is that I was trying to get along with her. I'm sure her recollection is that she was trying to get along with me. And I know I was demented—a *lunatic*—except when I was on the phone trying to get enough jobs to keep the insurance going so that he could stay at home.

But one night it came to a head. I was never big on structure with Mikey, and this always drove her crazy, because during this time, I'd let him fall asleep without his pajamas on. I was in the bedroom once, and she called in, "Well, he's just a spoiled brat." I just stormed out. I just marched out of the house, without even taking my purse. I drove to Natalie's house, and all I had was my car keys. I didn't have a clue where to go. I've had this huge fight, and now what do I do? And then I had to go back. Well, I've got to go back, where else am I going to go?

So I go back, and Denny comes in—he was still able to get around—and he says, "Well, they're waiting for the cab. They're going home." So they left.

Laughter and Sorrow

Then Colleen O'Halloran arrived. She was his beloved cousin, and I'd always been a little jealous of her; they were *soooo* close. I'm not by nature a jealous person, but they were such soulmates. His mother wasn't nuts about her, because she had known that they had had a brief tryst in their youth, and felt they were going to wind up with three-headed children. But they had always been so close, and it did make me feel left out.

She was happy enough for him when we were married, but they remained so very close, and I never looked forward to the times when she was coming to town. But when Denny called her to tell her he had cancer, she quit her job and came to L.A. She was a nurse, and she did all the infusions, all the hook-ups. She was unbelievable. I will never be able to thank her enough.

Many other people helped, like my friend Rosanna, who would take Denny to the doctor. Sometimes my friend Charlie would take him. But Colleen did everything. She was even a great cook; a great vegetarian cook, and she would try to cook healthy food for him. What more could you ask for in the way of help? But I remember driving home one day and I saw this couple walking down the street with their arms around each other, laughing, and I said, "Isn't that great?" and then I realized it was Denny and Colleen, and I thought, "Well, where does that put me?" And they saw me, and they knew I saw them. I went home and I said, "I gotta tell you, it made me feel real sad. I just felt on the outside, here." And he said, "I know, I know."

But it hurt my feelings. I was trying to do so much, and I was feeling so sad and lonely and angry and isolated and overwhelmed and further away from Denny. Because everything he loved about me when he was well—my tenacity, my independence—really began to get on his nerves. His mother and father used to say about me, "You rile everybody up." And I do. I always thought that was a good thing. Dennis always thought that was a good thing. But if you're kind of low-key and going through an incredibly difficult time, I guess you don't want to be riled up.

Denny finally said to me, "Everybody else wants me to be comfortable. You just want me to live."

And I did, and I was just determined that he was going to live, at any cost.

A bunch of our wonderful friends planned a fundraising benefit for us. Jo Anne Worley booked a theater for the event. This description of the evening is taken from my 1992 Christmas letter:

> ... that incredible January night at the Pasadena Playhouse. It was called "An Evening of Friendship and Love for Dennis and Marcia" and, under the direction of Kimothy Cruse, our friends made it all happen, backstage, onstage and in the audience. Billy Barnes, Alan Bates, Leslie Easterbrook, Patrick Duffy, Lu Leonard, Bob Newhart, Suzanne Pleshette, Henry Polic, Brett Somers, David Steinberg, Lily Tomlin, The Great Tomsoni, Dawn Wells and Jo Anne Worley were all brilliant, and everybody stood up at the end of the show to acknowledge us, and I said, "It's okay if he gets well, isn't it?" and there was this giant roar of approval from five hundred people. It was truly a magic night.

It was like being there for your own memorial service.

Brett came into town. In and out. She would come, we'd fight, and then she would leave. And then she would come again. And my friend Brian Gibson would come over every morning for an hour or two and we would chant and do morning gongyo (prayers). And half the time we'd start to laugh, and couldn't stop laughing. At least once a week we would start howling, and everybody else in the house would start to laugh, and then everyone would laugh. I think that was probably even more important than the chanting.

Just Ignore the Guy in the Garden

During all of this, we were trying to sell the house. Poor Denny; when prospective buyers came to look, we took him, with all his IVs, out into the back garden, and he'd have to sit out there till they were gone.

Our health insurance was still in effect, but it's amazing what it won't pay; it won't pay for anything remotely experimental, remotely alternative. I packed Denny in the car and took him down to the Livingstone Clinic—it's an immunology center where they concentrate on boosting the immune system while you fight your cancer. The first day, he felt hopeful, he said, but basically, he was so very, very sick. When we arrived, I let him out at the entrance and left to park the car, and by the time I got back, he'd just gone up and down in the elevator; he couldn't find the floor.

He was taking various medications, but his digestive system was so compromised that very little of what could help him—or fuel him—could get through. It's a blockage. Conventional medicine doesn't do well with malabsorption; they just pump fat and sugar into your system through something called total parenteral nutrition, or TPN, which is a travesty, because it goes right through you. Meanwhile, the pancreas and liver weren't performing their functions of cleansing, getting rid of the toxins and everything. And none of that nutrition was going in, so I watched him lose his body mass, not just weight.

That was one of the things I didn't want to hear from the surgeon. The surgeon said, "He'll probably die of malnutrition." I said, "Fuck you. Don't be giving me no bad news. It's possible; he can make it." And Denny always said, "I wish we hadn't done the chemo." The chemo and the radiation lasted for several weeks; but the point is, he'd get dehydrated, and it didn't help. It doesn't always help with a tumor. Chemo can help a lot with something like lymphoma or leukemia, systemic things. But tumors it doesn't do well. It really doesn't.

We tried so many things. We had a healer; we did Chinese medicine. And his treatment got rid of the tumor in his pancreas, but it's so close to the liver, it just jumped right over to the liver. We tried organic juices, vitamins—I can't go near a carrot now, to this day. I can't go near juice. I had this big board up there of all the Chinese medicine and the vitamins and everything, and finally Denny said, "Leave me alone. Every time I open my mouth you're trying to get something in."

It took pounds of carrots to make this carrot juice. His mother refused to do it. She felt it was a futile gesture and wouldn't help. She felt I was forcing him to do things and preventing the inevitable. Finally I said, "You think he's going to die, don't you?"

"Yes," she said, "the *family* does."

That made me feel even more isolated. And they thought I was making him uncomfortable, and that I was making him sad, and trying to beat a dead horse, and I wasn't on board. So I felt more and more lonely and more and more isolated. I was going out there, doing whatever I could do—horrible jobs, horrible jobs—to just keep him in that house, which I did. I kept him in our house. And somehow I got that little boy to school. Even though by this time he was wandering around the house at night, going to sleep wherever he could.

Denny ran fevers in the middle of the night, always—phantom fevers—and I often had to take him to the emergency room. Nobody was sleeping. So nights were just the proverbial nightmare.

Then Colleen went home again. She left because Winifred wanted to come back; she had had some distance from the situation, and now she was ready to come back again. At the time I had an acting job in New York, and I was thrilled to have to go. Brett and I went to see *Crazy For You*, and we had the best night, and I stayed with my dear friend Carol Richards. But when I came home, there was a call from Doug, Denny's brother, saying that Denny was in the hospital. I look back on it now, and as much as I feel I failed him, I did keep him in our house, I stayed up with him, I got his fever down.

Even if I was demented. Maybe I wasn't demented; maybe I was just determined.

I came home to have another fight, a really huge fight. My mother-in-law said, "I love him sixty thousand times more than you ever could." And I said, "Why are you so mean to me?" At this point I wanted Dennis to get out of his dying chair and beat her up. Which was so very enlightened of me. So she stormed out again. Went back home.

When Winifred left, Colleen came back. By now I was up twenty-four hours a day, and I just couldn't do it alone. The great thing about medical care, managed care—they won't put you in the hospital unless it's less expensive than to keep you at home. He wasn't in a hospital bed, but he looked like he was there; he had all the IVs, because they had to pump all that stuff into him. He would often get dehydrated, then he'd need transfusions of saline solution. He had the Hickman catheter in his chest, and he often had to have that changed, and had to have the stent changed pretty frequently, so he wouldn't turn yellow again. Through all this Colleen was absolutely great.

But she had said to me from the first, "You have to let him go." And I said, "Screw you; it's too soon, and leave me alone." Talk about not wanting to hear this. She said that from the beginning Denny had said, "You've got to help me if I need you to; you've got to help me die." And she said to me, "Can you do it?" And I said, "No." And I was astonished that I said no, but I said, "No, I can't." I was still going out there, doing my very best; still hoping, somehow, "We're going to pull this out." That's the good part and the bad part of being a metaphysician; somehow, I've got to make this happen.

15 don't look back

→

Dying Husbands, Real Estate and the L.A. Riots

Memorial Day came. We've always done barbecues with some of my friends from my David Craig class. Denny said he wanted them to come. Now, the thing that was hardest for Dennis was that he loved to cook and he loved to eat, and from the minute he was diagnosed, he couldn't even stand to be in the kitchen; it made him nauseous. He didn't want to eat, and I was trying to shove food down him.

So, they all came over, our friends from David Craig's class. Denny had always cooked; he was the barbecuer. This time, Hugh Maguire barbecued. Everybody was pretending. They said, "Denny, come on, eat!" He piled the food on his plate, and then he just put it down and said, "Excuse me," and went in and went to bed.

By now my insurance brought in a night nurse. The first one was some sort of drug addict lunatic, and Colleen got her fired. But the second one was Sue Chandler, and she was an angel from above—an *angel*. The morning after the barbecue, Sue came in to me and said, "He wants to talk to you."

And Denny was sobbing, sobbing beyond belief—sobbing, sobbing, sobbing. And he said, "I'm dying. I can't cook a meal for my friends. I can't pick my son up. I can't take you out on our anniversary. I'm dying. And please don't make me feel like a failure." He wanted me to hold him, and I did, but not like I should have. There was some coldness in me, some anger in me. I couldn't pretend; how could I pretend? He said, "You can't make me take any more pills. You've got to get rid of *that*." I had this big chart, you know, of all the hundreds of pills and medications and vitamins I wanted him to take. I took the chart down.

Then a couple of days later we had this huge fight. *Huge* fight. "You hate me," he said. "I know you hate me, and I'm moving out."

"Fine!" I said. "Fine! Let me get you a cab!"

"No, I'll get a bus!"

And I thought, "This is not like the movies where everybody behaves so well and nobody gets upset." I mean, life is stressful enough; you put a terminal disease on top of that, and it just explodes through the roof! It was just unbearable.

Then a couple of days later was the Rodney King verdict, and I was out and about, listening to the car radio describing how they were rioting at the Beverly Center, which was pretty nearby. The traffic was insane. When I finally got home, he said, "I was so worried about you. Where were you? I feel so useless, I feel so helpless; I can't protect my family." And I saw how he was so sad. I was so full of sadness and rage and impotence and terror, I just thought, "Start up with me, come on"—the rioters, I mean—"I'd love it. Come on, you guys want a fight?" I couldn't have been less afraid. I was *so* not afraid. I was so enraged. Right around our block, our particular neighborhood, whole blocks were burned, but ours was spared.

When I think about what Mikey was going through—armed soldiers on the corner, his father getting sicker and weaker every day, all these people coming through the house ... we were still trying to sell it.

By now, Denny was in a hospital bed and we couldn't send him out into the yard anymore when people came to look at the house. Besides all the IVs, he had a catheter. Denny never liked wearing clothes; he would have been perfectly happy nude most of his life. But once he was diagnosed, he couldn't have clothes on. He was constantly taking them off. "Dennis, could you put on your—" "No, I can't. I can't put on my clothes. I can't!"

So, picture this, if you will: "Okay, honey, the realtor's just going to show us a nice house on Genesee." You walk in the front door, and there in the living room is the nude dying guy hooked up to his IVs, and this demented woman from *The Bob Newhart Show*: "Hello, how are you? Is there anything I can show you?"

I look back on it now and howl. I mean, there I was, crazy as a loon. Did I think nobody was going to notice the dying guy sitting in the living room hooked up to endless IVs? The sicker he got, the fewer clothes he wanted to wear, which made for an even more *bizarre* scene. Many people never made it past the living room, in case there were more dying naked guys in the back of the house.

Nobody ever made an offer (what a shock) and we were fired by our real estate agent. Which turned out to be a good thing, because somehow I managed to keep the house.

Mikey was going to Play Mountain Place School then, a wonderful, nurturing school, and one evening there was a parents' meeting. Everyone was taking turns talking about their concerns, and when it was my turn I said, "I don't know how I'm going to be able to bear it when my darling dies." And of course everybody started to sob. We were all sobbing, and sobbing, and sobbing—but it was the first time I'd ever said it out loud.

My friend Baillie Vigon had given us the gift of referring us to Dr. Ann Kirsch. Ann saw all three of us, and I don't know what we would have done without her. Shortly after this parent meeting, Ann came to the house. She'd come over to see Mikey, and Mikey wasn't there, so I made her help me turn Dennis. He kept trying to get out of bed. There's poor Ann—this is not in a psychologist's line of duty; I mean, imagine how she must have felt—there's this emaciated dying guy, hallucinating, *nude*, and I'm asking her to flip him over in the bed!

Anyway, I told her what I'd said at school; that I didn't think I'd be able to stand it. And she told me that Denny had said to her,

"Everybody thinks Marcia's going to be fine, but she's not. She's not going to be fine at all. And you've got to help her." He knew better.

Denny had so much courage. He never said, "Why me?" He never said, "It's not fair." He never said, "How can I stand this?" He was just such a classy guy. He was totally fearless. He said, "I have loved you, without condition—it just wasn't long enough. But I can't bear that I'm not going to be able to see Mikey growing up." And he wrote him a letter, which I'll show you later.

Denny's Last Requests

The week before he died, he said to me, "Look, I want a party."

By this time I knew enough to honor his feelings. There we were: he was sitting in his chair and I was sitting on the couch, and he's saying, "I want good champagne, and don't be giving them no chips. I want good food, good champagne. And I want a celebration, like Judy had." (Judy Thomas had died six months earlier, and he was still well enough then to go to her funeral. It was like a celebration of her life. He really liked that.) "Just toast me in the backyard," he said. And he told me who he wanted there, and he said to ask Charlie Cilona and Guy Birster if they'd cook his favorite food from their restaurant.

I said, "Okay. Okay." But when I look back now, I think what we did was very rare, because most people don't have the courage to do that, or even talk about it. Or even admit what the reality is.

Then he said, "I want to be cremated, and I want you and Mikey to take the ashes and go up to Big Sur. And don't take a lot of people with you."

I mean, he was days from death, but he was looking out for me. And he was, of course, totally right. "I want you to pick a great spot and scatter my ashes," he said.

Not long after that, I'm sure he had a stroke, which often happens with very terminal cancer patients. He was hallucinating; he started to call out for his mom.

It was a Friday, the day that Ann and I were trying to get him back in bed, and I'm *still* in total denial, like this is the most normal thing in the world, and he's in what Mikey calls the "dying room," but it's the *dining* room. Then Saturday he started to become very anxious. The doctors, they tell you they'll make you comfortable; they don't.

There's anxiety in dying. Enormous anxiety. It's not peaceful at all. *At all.* And he's calling out. And there's a death rattle—there actually is, from this tremendous phlegm that gathers in the throat. Sue said to me—we were up all night, and it was scary, it was very scary—and she said, "You know, you don't have to do this. You don't. It's perfectly all right if you can't do this; we'll take him to a hospital." And I said, "No, he doesn't want to go." And then, somehow, after this unbearable thirty-six hour period, he just went into a coma.

But there were people in and out all day, like there wasn't this dying guy in the dining room. Friends of mine in and out, Gary Dontzig and Gary Campbell, and I remember laughing. *Laughing!* There were a bunch of us sitting in the living room just laughing like none of this was happening.

Our friend Jeffrey Josephson had taken Mikey. His father had committed suicide when he was eight, so he knew what it was like to be a kid losing your dad. He took Mikey and he said, "Now, you call me when this happens."

Everybody left about four o'clock, and I went in and sat down next to Denny. Now, I had been telling him, "It's okay. It's okay to go." Because clearly this was a guy who would have died months earlier—he was ready, he wasn't afraid—but he was waiting for me. So I sat down beside him. It was just the two of us; Colleen was sleeping in the bedroom. And I said, "Okay, Denny." And he took three really deep breaths, and he died. It was unbelievably peaceful, and precious. He was waiting for everybody to leave.

So I'm sitting there, holding his hand, feeling his presence in the room, feeling his great relief at being out of that body. And my relief. To watch somebody rot before your eyes—someone with such vitality; Dennis was so virile—such a strong, vital guy. And I'm sitting there, just feeling him, and the doorbell rings, and it's the twenty-five dollars' worth of Thai food I had ordered! That's a lot of food. It's not easy to spend twenty-five dollars on Thai food. And I actually did say to Denny, "You're dead three minutes, and I've got food at the door!"

In my defense, at least I didn't eat it.

I went to the back room and I said to Colleen, "He's dead." And she looked very shocked, very unnerved, very strange. Two years later, she told me that she had been saving enough morphine to kill him. And that he had asked her to, and that she was going to do it that day. But somehow Denny hadn't wanted her to have to do that. There was something so sweet about that. She wanted to do it for him, and he didn't want her to have to live with that act. And I was so grateful that I didn't have to do anything along those lines.

Denny always made it very clear that he wanted to be cremated and not have any expensive funeral, not that we had the money anyway. We always planned to call the Neptune Society, which cremates people and gives you the ashes or scatters them at sea. Now, my sister Sherry had made it her business to make sure everything would be ready. She said, "You've got to make arrangements; you've got to sign this Neptune Society thing." And she finally forced me to do it. It was only signed a week before he died, but it saved us from an autopsy, and from having to call people, and from unbelievably stressful stuff. And I got a refund! Right after he died, they said, "Dear Mrs. Hawley, you get a rebate, because your loved one died within a certain amount of time." He died soon enough so you get a rebate! Please! Just one more bit of insanity.

So then "the Blues Brothers" showed up. The Neptune Society actually, but they looked exactly like the Blues Brothers. They have those thin black ties and those black shirts. But no sunglasses. "Hi, there. We're from the Neptune Society."

But before they arrived, I had called Jeffrey and he brought Mikey home to see his dad.

The Monday before he died, I had come out to the dining room, and there they were, Denny and Mikey, wrapped around each other.

Mikey had his arms around Denny's neck, and they were just holding on to each other for a very long time. And they didn't know I'd seen them.

The one thing I couldn't watch was them zipping Denny up and taking him out. By this time, I was kind of euphoric. I was so happy for him, that he was out of that body. I hadn't even begun to feel the loss.

I called everybody: "Well, this is Marcia Wallace. Thank you for everything you've done, and Dennis has died today..." I had come kicking and screaming to the realization that I had to let him go. I would still be trying to push food into his mouth. But that's something you just can't do. You cannot force somebody to eat when they don't want to. And god knows I tried. He wanted to hide when he saw me coming. He was so relieved when he finally said to me, "You have to let me go."

And I said, "I will."

16 don't look back

In Pieces

So we had a wonderful party. Denny's parents and his sister had gone back home, but my brother and my sister were there, all Denny's friends from San Francisco, our mutual friends like Hugh and Ruth McGuire, whom he really loved. Just very close friends, probably thirty people. It was very personal. It was a beautiful day, a wonderful party; it was exactly what he wanted.

I had said to my friend Rosanna Levinson, who was devoted to Dennis, "We can just do plastic champagne glasses." And everybody whirled on the widow. "Excuse me? Excuse me? Dennis Hawley's memorial? We will have *real* champagne glasses." Which, of course, was as it should be.

Rosie provided those, and Charlie and Guy's food was superb. Their restaurant had been Denny's favorite, and they fixed all his favorite dishes. Denny had planned the menu himself—he was the greatest host in the world—eggplant tart, frisée salad with bacon and potatoes, beef with Béarnaise sauce, crème brûlée. And Charlie and Guy cooked it all superbly. *"Don't be giving them no chips."* He was the host to the end.

Mark Goldberg brought cases of Denny's favorite champagne, and after the meal we all went out to the garden and talked about Denny and offered toasts. Jo Anne sang "Our Love Is Here To Stay."

His friend Jim Newcom talked about going to football games with him. That's when I said, "Ladies and gentleman, this is Mrs. Norman Maine." I was just demented. I read the letter he wrote to Mikey, and the poem he'd written to me:

> *To my beloved Marcia on Christmas, 1990.*
> *My darling, we've come to the end of the year,*
> *And through all of our problems, we still have*
>   *good cheer.*
> *For richer for poorer, in sickness and health*
> *Got stretched to the limits, and still we have wealth.*
> *Our darling, our Michael, the joy of our life,*
> *And you, my sweet Marcia, my beautiful wife.*
> *You inspire me and love me, you're my life's*
>   *dream come true.*
> *Through my mood-swings and pouting your sweetness*
>   *shines through.*
> *I will love you forever, and eternally be*
> *Truly grateful to have you and Mikey love me.*
> *Merry Christmas, my darling, the joy of my life.*
> *Happy New Year, my sweetheart, my wife.*

My friend Allison said to me that day, "I was having a terrible time with Denny's death, and then I figured, God knew what was coming, and he sent him you." I don't believe the way she does, but that was so *sweet.* You can substitute "universe" for God, or "the boddhisatvas," or whatever, but the thought is the same: We knew it was coming and We sent him you. This was a very comforting concept. But I think for a while I was feeling mainly relief. Of course, I didn't know what was to come: the terrible, excruciating grieving process. But that day, I thought, "Oh, I've done most of my grieving; I'm going to be fine."

Colleen had gone and gotten Denny's ashes from the Neptune Society, and we put them on a small round end table. Then we put some flowers there too, and found his eyeglasses, and his favorite apron, and you know, we started putting all sorts of his favorite things there, and some photos. Mikey named it "the Daddy Table," and we kept that going for a long time.

And then, after the amazing memorial, we all caravanned up to Big Sur with Denny's ashes. He was right, of course; I should have gone up there with Mikey alone, because there was a whole bunch of us and it was pretty awful.

We stopped off at San Luis Obispo to have lunch at the Madonna Inn, which was a favorite place of ours, and we started telling stories, and I remember I was driving, and I thought, "Well, this is fine. This is going to be fine." hen Brett started sobbing; Brett sobbed for about an hour in the car. And Mikey slept all the way up. But I still thought, "Well, it's going to be fine."

And we got up there and started to look for a good place to scatter the ashes, and then somebody made the mistake of saying, "Look, I really have to get back." And I just lost it. All this anger and frustration and sadness and everything just blew up, and I said, "Give me a damn minute here. What do you want me to do, throw him in the street?! I'm going to find the perfect place." And it got incredibly tense, and I remembered Denny saying, "Just you and Mikey go. Just you and Mikey go." Brett was great; she was trying to calm everyone down. So was Sherry. And I was yelling at Mikey. But I was determined.

I looked around the Ventana Inn, which is where we spent so many anniversaries, and was a place Denny loved so much, and finally we ended up in Pfeiffer Park. Now, who's to know it's against the law to scatter ashes? You can only do it at sea; I didn't know. So I start looking around and looking around, and by now nobody's speaking to me. Even Colleen, after all this time and all this closeness between us, wasn't speaking to me either. (I'm so grateful that was only temporary). I couldn't believe it; I had all these people who weren't speaking to me. But of course what it was was rampant raging grief that nobody knew what to do with, and it was just so painful and so awful.

But I stuck to my guns and found this glorious spot in Pfeiffer Park. I've been back often, and Denny's brother, who hasn't spoken to me since then, goes there all the time. It's a clearing surrounded by enormous redwoods, beside a very deep brook. So you hear the sound of the water and you can see the sun coming through the redwoods; it was glorious, absolutely glorious. So that was it, with everybody not speaking, and everybody in pain. We all took—it was mostly Mikey and me—everybody took handfuls and scattered Denny's ashes. And then people started getting real busy with their watches again, and I said, "What, are you people in a hurry here?" And I lost it again. People left in droves. The grief was choking us all.

But Mikey and I were there in Big Sur where Denny and I had spent so many wonderful times. It was our place, and we loved it so. And I was able to do that for him. I was totally nuts, but I was able to do it. For my darling. For Dennis.

So Denny had his ashes sprinkled around in this beautiful clearing. (When Charlie went there a few months later, it still hadn't rained, and he told me you could still see them on the redwoods.) And we sprinkled rose petals; it was a wonderful ritual for us. Mikey enjoyed it; it was really important for him. It would have been much more traumatic for him—although maybe much better for Dennis—if Denny had died of a heart attack. I was still feeling euphoric that he wasn't in pain anymore; and I felt his spirit, very definitely leaping around, free from that body. I felt him so close to me.

My Angel

It was a great love, a great love affair that we had, me and Denny. And the testament is Mikey, because he's such a great kid. He still hasn't read the letter from his dad yet, but he will when he's ready. I have a deep conviction that our lives are eternal, that it is just like waking and sleeping, that we are born together with the people we love lifetime after lifetime. I really do believe that Dennis and I will be together again, that we'll always be together, and that next lifetime it will be perfect. I mean, how much more "karma" can there be to expiate?!

That's what he said in the letter, that we'll all be together again. And his handwriting is so clear; he's so closely connected to me. He's my guardian angel. I don't believe in much anymore, but I believe in Denny. He's not going to take himself away. He's waiting; he's hanging here to watch over us, protect us, be close to us. It's just too intense a love to have been just six years and then nothing. It's very deep.

Like I say, my relationship with the Hawleys was pretty much in shambles after that. His parents had been such a help when he was dying, but we grew further and further apart. I so wish we'd been able to reach out to each other during this awful, awful time. But we couldn't.

Friends used to say to me, "You're my hero; you're doing so great." But I wasn't. I loved him so much and there were times when I just let him down. Oh, I kept the wolf at bay, the house out of foreclosure one day at a time, and tried to keep some continuity in Mikey's life. But so often I was just isolated in my rage and grief and sadness. *I did not want him to die!* And I kept thinking, "Please, please, there must be something more I can do," so I was always coming at him with carrot juice and vitamins and potions and treatments, and sometimes I just forgot to hold him and cry with him, and just *be* in the time we had left. I so regret that. And he knew.

After the memorial, Mikey and I left town. I went to do *The Odd Couple* in Missouri, and I did *Steel Magnolias* again. I was on the road for months, so in many ways it was as if Denny wasn't dead, because I was away from home as I often was, especially that last year when he wasn't working. This job went off and on for about six months. And after it was all finished, I walked back into the house one day and went to pieces. Totally.

Christmas 1992

Dear friends,

     I dedicate this Christmas letter to my beloved husband, Dennis Hawley, who died of pancreatic cancer on a Sunday in June. He died with his usual dignity and humor, after fighting this deadly malignancy for seven months. Dennis and I always believed the mind, body and spirit work together in any healing process. We also believed that somebody has to be that two percent of people who survive this particular cancer, and why shouldn't he be one of those people? This was our approach. We didn't know any other way to begin this journey. And I know we'd do it the same way again.

     I'm nowhere near the end of this experience of grief and loss—that big wrecking ball crashes into my heart daily. But I am moving forward and I really wanted to write this letter. I wanted to reach out to all of you in profound appreciation for your friendship and generosity. The support was spectacular. His beloved parents were here in a flash and did everything; his cousin and dear friend, Colleen, took a hiatus from her job as a nurse in Hawaii to come help us; my sister, as always, was the one I called when I was falling apart; my brother Jim took a second job on Saturday fifty miles from his home to send us the money; my mother, who loved Dennis with all her heart, wrote him regularly.

     And our friends, our fabulous friends, people like yourselves—you did so much. It meant more than you can ever know. You gave us your time, your money and your hearts. You made us food and you made us laugh. You gave me work and you gave Dennis rides to endless doctors, and you listened to us both. You cared for Mikey, and you cared about him. You called and you visited and you cared deeply about Dennis's life. He knew that, and it touched his heart.

     Everybody who knew Denny knew he considered regrets to be a giant waste of time. Why look back, we're not going that way. And he was not afraid to die. Please don't misunderstand, he did not want to leave us, and he fought—oh, how he fought—until he couldn't anymore. It was very hard for me to let go; I had become this spiritual pit bull. But he woke me up at four in the morning on Memorial Day and said, "I can't do this anymore." I said, "Okay."

Ten days later, at about four o'clock on an absolutely beautiful Sunday afternoon, I sat down next to him and took his hand and said, "It's time. It's time to go to the light, and it's okay. You didn't let anybody down, and we will love you forever." He took three deep breaths and died. I know that he waited for me, and this probably seems like an odd word to use, but it was the most precious moment of my life. Mikey came into the room and said, "Is my dad dead?" and I said, "Yes, honey," and he said, "Well, let's call the firemen and they'll pour water on him and he'll grow again."

His awareness has been astonishing, this child of Dennis Hawley, this Michael (don't call me cute, call me cool) Wallace Hawley. Before his dad died, we were looking at family pictures, and I said, "There's Daddy," and he said, "No, that's my other dad, that's my well dad." After he died, Mikey said to me, "Mom, my dad's spirit is in the universe, right?" and I said yes, and then a lamp flickered in the room, and he put his hands on his hips and said, "DAMN."

He was having trouble cutting a pumpkin, and one day when I picked him up at school, he said, "Mommy, Mommy, I cut my pumpkin all by myself. You know what? Something happened in my brain and my Dad helped me." Last week, I was crying and he said, "Mom, don't be sad" and I said, "Well, I am sad, honey; I miss Daddy," and he said, "Can't you be just a little happy? I know we can't be happy Daddy died, but can't you be happy nobody chopped down all the trees today?" And you know what? I could.

I know this letter is way too long, but I didn't know how to condense such a life-altering experience; it somehow diminishes the life and death of this extraordinary man. And I didn't just want to talk about him, I wanted to include something of him, by him.

Dennis Hawley was hands-down the best parent I ever saw. Here's the letter he wrote to his beloved boy before he died.

To my dearest Michael,

Both your mother and I believe that life is eternal and that the soul and the spirit never die. We believe that the love we have for each other as a family... a mother, a father and a son ... will live forever. We believe this so strongly that it somehow makes Daddy's death easier to understand and more a part of what life is about. You're the only child I ever had and if I got to pick from all the children in the world I couldn't find anyone more wonderful than you. I wish there was something your mother and I could have done to prevent this terrible tragedy and I know it will be many years before you get over the loss of your dad. I just want you to know how special you have been to me... no one else could ever take your place and the years since you were born have been among the best and happiest years of my life. I will always be there watching over you and our special connection will never be broken. I told this to your mommy and she typed it for me, but it is from my very heart and soul and I will love you and your mommy every day of your beautiful lives.

Daddy

I loved Dennis Hawley more than I've ever loved anyone, and rightly so; he made my life sing. As long as this heart of mine beats, my Denny, my wonderful Denny, lives there.

17 don't look back

Our House

Time to go back to Ann Kirsch again. Ann was a former teacher who became a therapist. Denny saw her, I saw her, and Mikey saw her. With kids, she'd get down on the floor, and she had all these toys to act out the hospital stuff and stomach stuff. Mikey never knew he was in therapy. She was just helping him heal and helping him be part of what was going on. Which kids have never in the past been allowed to do.

Rosie O'Donnell was very up-front talking about this. She was ten when her mother was dying, and nobody ever told her. They had Rosie move out. Her mother died. Rosie came back. And all her mother's stuff had been taken away. Imagine—Rosie comes home, her mother is gone, no one talks about her anymore. I don't know if she was even allowed at the funeral. This is monstrous, except that's how it was done then. Even now, with us, people said. "Mikey's too young. He doesn't know what's going on; it'll just scare him." I knew that wasn't true. To *not* know is terrifying. The truth never hurt anybody, if you can make yourself face it.

Mikey's great fortune, too, was to have Gail Price as his teacher at Play Mountain. She was a tremendous support. Early on, she took me aside and said, "Look, when I was ten, my mother died and nobody ever talked to me; nobody ever told me. My mom would come home from chemo treatments and go to her room, shut the door and cry, and I thought I'd done something wrong. It shaped my life. You must make your child a part of this process; it's a family journey. People think kids are too young to understand it; that is all absolutely untrue. You may have to do it on their level, but you must do it."

This was extremely hard for Denny. He always said, "I love Marcia deeply and truly—we just didn't have enough time; but I can't bear leaving Mikey." I urged him to write that letter, and I asked him to talk to Mikey about what was coming. It seemed so important to me, because Denny had played with Mikey and talked to him and fed him and hugged him and read to him every day of his life; what, he's not going to notice if that stops? And when Denny did talk to him about the future, he was great. I really believe that his connecting with Denny at that time is the reason Mikey is so "together" about his father's death and has been able to cope so well.

Everyone at Play Mountain Place School helped. If they'd done nothing else but be there for him and me when Denny died, it would have been enough. They suspended school activities the day after he died, and I came to school, and people talked about how they felt, and the kids did sympathy cards, and they sent them all to me. That was a wonderful comfort. This kind of nurturing is what they do best.

It was Carol Potter, the mother of Mikey's friend Chris, who told us about Our House. Chris's dad died when he was nine months old. His mother had remarried by now, but she told me she had been to a bereavement group at Steven Weiss Temple, and it had really helped her, so I called, and we went. It was such a smart move. We were in the group about a year and a half. They eventually went off on their own and started their own bereavement center.

The Nature of My Grief

For many many years there was no such thing as bereavement. We don't handle death well in this country. When people talk about "closure," usually the person's only been dead for a week. When they say "So-and-so is doing very well," what they mean is, "They're not making *me* uncomfortable." But I found out that grief is not a linear process; you can go up and down so much in the same day—anger, denial, bargaining, acceptance, back to anger—you get whiplash.

For a long time there were only occasionally groups at churches for people who had been married fifty years and whose husbands or wives had died in their sleep. But more and more young people were dying and leaving young children, and there was no place for the widows and the kids to go. So this was the very first group in Southern California for young widows and widowers, started by Joann Lautman. I was certainly the oldest one there, but I qualified because Mikey was five. We had about twelve people in our group. More women go than men, but we had quite a few men in our group. Mikey went to his own group. Kids deal with grief mostly through art; they're encouraged to draw and write and stuff like that, and to play.

I realize that I was determined as a Buddhist to try to deal with death in an enlightened way. When Denny died, I felt him leaping around—I felt his *life* literally leaping. The day he died was one of the most beautiful days I've ever seen. And for him to be out of that body, the relief was immense.

But a couple of days before he died, I had a dream. When he was well and working, I used to lie in bed—he used to leave very early, and he'd turn the closet light on—and I'd watch him get dressed. By now it had been months since he had been able to wear belts or clothing because of the incredible, unbearable pain around his middle and his back. But in this dream, he was getting ready for work, and he was so buoyant and happy, although he still looked incredibly sick. But he was putting on a belt and a shirt and tie, and I, in my ever-present state of denial even in my dream, thought, *"That's it, he's cured."* But of course it was a dream about being ready to move on. And very sweet, really. Because it wasn't a dream of fear. He was ready, and he was dressed. And his belt didn't hurt him. And he died in two days. So on some level, I was ready, too.

But I don't know how people get through this experience without some kind of spiritual support. Well, they don't. It's a bad country for dying. You see it now; after the Columbine High School massacre, the talk was all closure, closure, closure. This was only two days after it happened! If only it were that simple. Those kids will be haunted as long as they live. Will they have good days? Of course. Will they go on to be happy? Of course. But it's not that simple. The media sound-bite mentality is that we have to quickly end the grieving, we have to have *closure*.

Some cultures know better how to grieve. Judaism, for example, allows a year, at least, before you're supposed to move on. The fact is, people get *remarried* while they're still grieving. It's not a linear journey; you feel bad and then you feel better and then you're fine. You can have months and years go by, and then all of a sudden you'll walk down the street and something triggers it. Six years later I was humming to myself in the car, and all of a sudden I had a memory, and I had to pull over because I was crying so hard.

Luckily I gave myself that. It can't be clean and neat. How can somebody have that place in your life and then be plucked out of that place, and it all heals up? It's not possible. Sometimes I think—and a couple of people have actually said to me, "Marcia, isn't it *time*?" I've gone about my life, I'm fun a lot of the time, I'm not morose, but I know people think that I've stayed stuck with Denny. What can I tell you? Maybe I've flunked widowhood. But I just loved him completely, and I always will. I'll always miss him.

In terms of Mikey, I have made enormous mistakes but I did two things extremely well: I handled the adoption well, and I handled Dennis's death very well. I hope, anyway, that those two things will eclipse anything else I handled badly. They're two biggies, *biggies*, because they're the sort of things that can haunt you forever.

During those first six months after Denny died, Mikey dealt with it pretty well. He had Ann Kirsch to talk to. And he and I spoke about Denny a great deal. There was a little light on Dennis's table and it used to flicker; Mikey thought that was his daddy. I tried to explain. It was very important to me to help him understand that his dad had returned to the universe and his spirit lived on.

But he would say, "Yeah, but he's in *heaven*, right?" And I realized that kids need their loved ones to be someplace, like Cleveland. They want it to be someplace specific. I'm not a big "heaven" fan, but I thought, let him have that. The other thing was just too much for him. Even though he liked the idea of the flickering light, and that somehow his dad helped him—he got the spirit of that—he still wanted him to have a home base.

When Denny was dying, all the discipline I could enforce was "You have to brush your teeth and you have to wear a seat belt." That was all I could do. I knew it was important to be consistent; as I said, I know made terrible mistakes. I felt so bad for Mikey that I bought him way too much stuff, which set a precedent that was in nobody's best interest, and I was warned about that. But I did what I did. Luckily, the more distance I got from Dennis's dying, the more I realized how deranged I had been.

I *felt* like I was functioning, but every once in a while I'd lose it. One day Brett snapped at me and I started to sob. I cried for days. I was unhinged. There were people—friends who I knew loved me—who said, "You're going get over this, aren't you? Denny wouldn't want you to feel bad." I said, "Trust me, he wouldn't mind if I cried a little." ("Oh, gee, I forgot all about that guy I was married to.")

People don't mean to, but they want to distance themselves: "All right, we've given you enough time; get over it." The sad thing is everybody's there with their casseroles, hundreds of people there with you on the day. And you really appreciate it. But then it tapers off. And when you need them the most, everybody's gone.

One day my friend Baillie Vigon, one of the David Craig group, called and said, "I know what a mess you are; I'm coming over there and we're going to clean out Mikey's room." So many gifts, so many friends.

Oddly enough, I had no trouble getting rid of Dennis's stuff. But I couldn't get his family to take anything. His brother took his jacket and I gave away some expensive ties. I kept a ring and some cufflinks for Mikey.

Even though some well-meaning people said to me, "You've got to move on," it's not possible, and it's not wise. Where there are children involved, these memories become the fabric of their lives. Dennis Hawley shaped the kind of man Mikey is going to become, even though Mikey can't remember now what he looked like. But he remembers certain things. One day he said, "I'm going to start drying myself off like Daddy dried himself off," and he did. He would bring his towel down to his feet; he wouldn't lift his feet up. I had forgotten that, but somehow Mikey—because they'd spent so much time together and used to take showers together—remembered it.

About eight months after Denny died, I had to have surgery on my stomach. Now, Mikey's perception was, Daddy went to the hospital with a stomachache and he died. I was afraid, too. I needed this relatively minor surgery, but I was incredibly scared to do it. For me, to this day, to go into a hospital and smell those smells—it is such a visceral thing, I really lose my balance. And at that point I just couldn't bear it. So from the minute I went in to have that surgery, we turned to Ann. She was so helpful; out came the hospital toys, and Mikey dealt with his fear that I was going to die, too.

Our House continued to be amazingly helpful. The wonderful thing about this group was that you could say *anything* there. We were all going through the same process, the same anger and frustration, and we knew how hard it was to talk about it. You need to be around people who've shared your experience.

People say the damnedest things, desperately trying to explain what happened, have it make sense. They hope whatever caused the death of that person, it's something *they're* not doing. Somebody actually said to me, voice lowered, hand on my arm, "Well, Dennis ate a lot of butter, didn't he." That's right, hon, you got it—butter killed him.

Another one of my favorite platitudes: "Well, at least you had him." And that's true. *Now* I can say that, but I didn't want to hear it then. And I didn't want to hear how lucky I was to have Mikey. That's true, too. But back then I was so damn sick of hearing how "lucky" I was, and I felt so incapable of dealing, I always wanted to say to them: "Fine! You come and raise him all by yourself!" I remember one time a woman whose husband had committed suicide said, "I'd give my daughter to have my husband back." Now, she didn't mean that, but the point is you could say anything and nobody would judge you, because everybody understood; everybody had been in those dark places.

You didn't have to be at your best, you see. You didn't have to behave; you could say things that would shock people. And they *would* shock people, because nobody in the real world wants it to happen to them, so they want you to be strong—for you and for them—and they don't want to hear about the anger you feel when somebody you love dies. They say, "Well, it's not their fault." Of course it's not their fault; of course it's not! But that's beside the point.

I was in the group intensely for about a year. One of the couples there even got married, and I was very happy for them. There are four or five of us widows who still get together and have dinner. Some members went on to other relationships—people started dating and stuff—but I was just stuck. I was in the throes of menopause, too; always great fun.

Denny was right; I certainly did need help, and not just in the immediate aftermath. I mean, years down the line, I still "lost it." The first year, you're kind of in shock; the second year you think you're going to be fine, and then something happens, and it starts all over again, only worse. It's not a linear journey, and it never really ends. It doesn't mean you can't be happy; it doesn't mean you can't go on; it doesn't mean you can't experience life. But for me, something in me closed up. Something that was always part of who I was. My optimism and my open heart. It did close down, and it ain't quite open yet.

But I'll keep trying.

18 don't look back

Unforgettable

My sister said something to me that I thought was hilarious. One day I had said, "Gee, I wish I were happier." And she said, "You've been happy!"

Now, she didn't think that was funny. She just thought that was true. She's right; I have been happy. I had real, genuine, drop-dead, take-your breath-away, light-up-your soul happiness. I've had that. Everybody deserves a miracle in their life, and mine was Dennis Hawley.

Not too long ago when people asked me how I was, I just wished they wouldn't, because I knew they didn't want to know and I didn't want to go into it. Now—and I consider it a real step forward—when people ask, "How are you?" I can say, "I'm fine. I'm okay." But for five or six years there when Dennis and I were together, I just thought, "Go ahead, ask me how I am so I can tell you. I'm fabulous. I'm wonderful. I can't stop smiling." This was a great gift.

It's not that I hadn't ever been happy before. I'd had some good times, some good laughs, some good friends, some good work, felt that sort of optimism, that "all's right with the world" feeling, before I met Denny. I think I had opened up to the possibilities of that happiness when I first became a Buddhist and started to chant. One day I was driving down Ventura Boulevard and tears sprang to my eyes and I was just hit with this unbelievable sense of well-being. This was totally new, in spite of all the good times and the good laughs—this sense of being one with the universe, of belonging. I think I had arrived at this point after a whole lot of hard work, so clearly I was ready for somebody like Dennis Hawley; we were ready for each other.

He got moody sometimes; it was sort of a pout. Not really a full-out pout, and it never lasted very long. The last year or year and a half of his life, though, he seemed to be more depressed. But he was sick. Who knew? But basically our relationship was so new for me, so unbelievable—it was so different from the relationship I had had with my parents. I'd stopped picking men who were like my mother. I'd given up my victim papers. And I was open to being cherished, and to cherishing someone else in return.

After all those years of being judged, he never judged me. My weight went up and down, and sometimes I'd see him look at me, and I'd think he must be thinking, "Oh, god, what happened to the woman I married?" But all he'd say was, "Oh, you're so pretty." There I was with no chin, shoving food in my mouth, and he was loving me and admiring me. It was always, "Do you mind if I cook this Thanksgiving? Would you be upset?" Not, "Jesus Christ, clean off the top of that refrigerator!"

I can't say enough about Denny. First of all, consider the romantic history that I had, starting with the guy with no teeth, and moving on to all those others, and thinking that the best I'd ever have was the legally blind therapist, the guy who'd always tell me that I didn't look good enough. And the wonderful thing about Denny and me? This was real life; it all held up. It was *real life*. And it never spoiled the way we felt about each other. That cold hard light of day, wrinkles and farts (and geese better scurry), we only loved each other more.

I suppose when people hear me talking about him, they think, "Well, she's simply deified that guy," and I don't mean to make him sound like a saint, because he wasn't, any more than I was. Or am. But he really was that great. Now, who's to know what might have happened seventeen years down the line; I'm sure we would have run into many snags. But that time we had together? When I'm really honest, it was every bit as fabulous as I thought it was at the time. Thank goodness I did appreciate it.

I know there are millions of single parents, women out there with less money than me, in crappy little apartments, but I can't help thinking, "You don't miss what you never had." I had this incredible love, this fantastic partner, so of course I'm going to miss it.

He made me laugh. He made me breathe. He taught me how to love. And I'll miss him till the day I die.

19 don't look back

On the Road Again

At the end of 1996, I realized that the bottom line was that I was still fat and Dennis was still dead, and I could only do something about one of those things. I didn't doubt that fat was what I had needed to be for all those long months, but I finally thought, "It's time." My moment of truth was an odd one. My friend Fred Ponzlov and I went to a Halloween party dressed as a reverse prom couple. It's one thing to be sort of a perky fat girl; it's another to look into the mirror and realize you look exactly like Wayne Newton on a really fat day. Scary... truly scary.

Shortly thereafter, a friend said, "Well, you have gotten a little hefty." Hefty? *Hefty?* I don't want to hear the word "hefty" unless we're talking garbage bags. So it was time to lose weight and open up my life a bit. You're ready when you're ready.

Something Else to Go Into Denial About

In the weeks after Denny's death, I either worked or lay on my couch and watched mindless talk shows. And we're talking *mindless* here. Let me put it this way: *Jerry Springer* was too intellectual for me. The day I realized I was no longer interested in alien lesbian grandmothers, I knew I was getting better.

I was still reeling with grief when I realized I was about to turn fifty. So I decided to hit the big five-oh in New York City. Joanie from my bereavement group said, "Hey, you'll be in New York, it's your birthday, you love steak (we covered a lot of topics in our grief group); you've got to go to Sammy's Roumanian Steakhouse." Well, okay, steak is steak, right? Romania, Nebraska, what's the diff? Sounds good to me.

So off we went: me, Brett, Carol Richards and Bill Schelble, close friends all. It was *waaaay* downtown, many dark stairs, and the first thing I noticed was that Sammy's lighting made me look like Margaret Thatcher's older sister. (Trust me, pick a restaurant with good lighting for your fiftieth birthday dinner.) There was one other table, occupied by eight people who had had *lots* of drinks. The birthday girl came over, sat on my lap, told me I was her favorite in all the world, she'd never loved anyone as much as me, she'd never forget this moment as long as she lived and then said, "My only regret is that I don't have my copy of your book 'Fried Green Tomatoes' with me so's you can sign it."

I didn't have the heart to tell her I wasn't Fannie Flagg.

In spite of the lack of business, it still took our waiter, Victor, who was only slightly younger than the Coliseum, hours to inch over to the table with his accordion to take our order. He served something gefilte and told the following joke: "My doctor asked me for a urine sample and a semen sample, so I gave him my shorts."

Hello, we're hoping to eat here. Then he coughed for thirty minutes. (By the way, he died last year and had a two-paragraph obituary in the *New York Times*. Go know.) When he put my plate down in front of me, I said, "Excuse me, I ordered the steak." He said, "Doll, this is the steak." It was gray and had been beaten within an inch of its life. Not unlike myself. I guess Sammy's is famous, but you couldn't prove it by me.

And then, adding to my list of unnerving experiences, I received the following via the mails: "Congratulations! You are now eligible to join the American Association of Retired Persons." Oh, thank you so much. Fifty, menopausal, a widow and now this? Demographically, I went from *Vanity Fair* to *Modern Maturity* in one fell swoop. Oh, well. Hopefully in my next life I'll get to the big events a little sooner, and won't be the only mom in my child's preschool with hot flashes.

Work was coming along, though, and I was able to keep my house (thank you Howard Borris). I did more *Simpsons* and other voice-overs, a recurring role on *Full House* and a role on *Murphy Brown* (thank you Gary Dontzig and Bob Newhart), for which I received an Emmy nomination. That upstart newcomer Eileen Heckart won, but what a thrill. I never really believed those people who said "It's an honor just to be nominated," but I'll be damned if it isn't true, and I enjoyed every minute of it.

There I was, attending the Emmy ceremony as a nominee, sitting in the audience among my fellow actors next to my "date" and beloved friend, Brett Somers, who was so overcome she started singing along with Bette Midler on "Rose's Turn." I kept hissing, "Brett, this is a live telecast." We were real popular in our row.

Also, I was on the cover of *Life* magazine in May 1994 as a breast cancer survivor, and began to speak about my experience to women around the country. Denny's death from such a deadly cancer made me more determined than ever to connect with as many women as I can to promote early detection, because this is a doable cancer.

Life With Mikey

Through it all there has been my Mikey. I am so crazy about this kid. He's kind and he's funny. He's incredibly tenacious (we call him Chile Relentless at our house), and he's ever so dramatic. (Gee, I wonder who he gets that from?) He told me the other day, "I just want you to know that this has been the worst day of my life. How could you do this to your only child?" I forget what I did, but I doubt it deserved a visit from Child Services.

And, as in all child-rearing, there's that constant process of having to eat crow (thus my continual weight problem). As he's grown older and begun to discover his body, I thought I would be as comfortable with those changes as I wanted him to be. Hah! One day in exasperation I blurted out, "Geez, Mikey, are you playing with yourself again?" and he said, "Mommy, it wants me to." And my wise reply? "I'm sure it does, dear." Oh well, I guess if we had one, we'd talk to it, too.

And as tough as it gets, somehow I never really feel that I'm raising this child alone, because who he is has been so shaped by those first four years with his dad, a truly extraordinary parent. Mikey also has his YoYo (the person, not the toy). That's what he calls my sister Sherry (for reasons unknown to all), who moved in with us after Denny died and has been such a help. I don't know what I would have done without her. Theirs is a truly mystical relationship. So here we are, a modern family for the new millennium, and you know what I always say: by the time he turns on me, I'll be deaf and won't be able to hear him anyway.

And the journey continues. I have my son, my friends and my work for which I'm so grateful. And now that I have some distance from the pain and despair of the immediate loss of my beloved husband, I'm so deeply grateful to have had Dennis Hawley in my life. He changed it forever. I loved and was loved. This wonderful man gave me unconditional positive regard and some people never experience that in ten lifetimes. And we had no regrets; it just wasn't long enough.

When Denny was dying, he said the most wonderful thing to me. He said, "I'm so glad we used our good china." And we did. It's such a beautiful metaphor for our life together, and when he died there was nothing unresolved or unexpressed. We didn't wait until tomorrow "to have a life," for which I'm so glad, because that life turned out to be way too brief.

When a loss like this happens, at first you're just falling and falling and falling. You have no balance, no bearings; you have nothing you can count on. Before, you're always saying, "That's not going to happen; that happens to other people." And when the worst possible thing that could happen happens, you'll never be the same again. I used to be a wildly optimistic person. But now I think because the worst happened once, it could happen again. You really have to be careful not to sit and wait for the other shoe to drop.

Voices

About a year after Denny died, I had a very interesting experience with James Von Praagh, who is now a very big deal. He's written all those books about The Other Side; he's a medium. As I mentioned earlier, my beloved manager Judy had died right before Dennis. One day her daughter (and my now agent) Annie Schwartz called me and said, "Listen, I heard about this 'medium' guy; here's his number." I called, but it was the wrong number. So I concluded that it wasn't the time for me to do it. But then Steve Lococo, who cuts my hair, also asked me if I'd ever heard of him, and he gave me the number. So, I called him and I made an appointment.

James was just a guy from Brooklyn. There were no lights or mirrors or "whooh-whooh" stuff. It was an amazing experience. And I never want to go again, because . . . I don't know why. It was actually very funny. He started out by saying, "Your husband's name was Dennis, right?" I said, "Oh, my god! Oh, my god!" He said, "Calm down; you told me already." But then he said, "Look, if the person on the other side believed in this, is open to this possibility, they're a lot easier to tap into. I'm just a conduit, you know; if somebody shows up, I'll just tell you what they say." And he didn't change his voice or anything like that. The lights were on; we were sitting in chairs.

He said my dad showed up first. It makes total sense that my dad would show up first and want to talk about himself. I wanted him to say, "I'm sorry I hit you, so sorry I hit you." He mentioned that. And he mentioned Dennis's Aunt Vi being there. She was his favorite aunt; he absolutely worshipped her. Then I said, "What about Judy?" And James told me she said, "Well, honey, it's about fucking time." Now, this is exactly what Judy would say. I said, "Ask her, was she surprised to die?" And he said she answered, "Honey, you could have knocked me over with a feather."

After Judy and my dad, Dennis came. James said things that nobody in a million years would know. He said, "Dennis loves that you wear his red terrycloth robe. And he loves that you made a table for him with the flowers and the pictures." You know, some naysayer said, "Oh, well, plenty of people have a table with flowers and pictures." But the terrycloth robe was pretty good.

Call it mumbo-jumbo if you want; the point is, whatever happens after you die, there's got to be a transitional period before you go on to your next step or next stage or come back or whatever it is you're going to do. So it made total sense to me. And it just made me feel so good. James got tears in his eyes when he spoke about Denny. He said he sensed that Dennis was a really handsome guy, but he had such sweetness about him, and he loved me so much. He picked up on all the special things about Denny, and got some very specific stuff. He said that Denny was fine, and I felt so comforted. I don't know how it worked and I don't care. I felt a lot better.

Holding it All Together

Meanwhile, even a year after Denny died, the debts kept mounting up. I hadn't been able to sell the house (dying guy in the living room and all). The house was in foreclosure twice, and I still owed the IRS the penalty from dissolving my retirement fund too early. Dennis hadn't worked for a year before he died. I wasn't working much, there was a ton of medical stuff insurance didn't pay for—it was overwhelming, just overwhelming. I wanted to climb under the covers and stay there. People said, "Let the house go." But I thought, "I'm not letting this house go. This was our dream house; I'm not taking Mikey out of this house."

I called everyone I knew in the business. I borrowed more money, but I needed to earn a lot more. Then I thought, "I've got to push the envelope of what I do. I'm not getting a new TV series, so let's just push the limits of how it's going to happen." I did some dialog looping for a while, which is background noise for movies and TV shows. Even though the audience can't really hear it, they want real conversations with real information. And then one day I was on the cover of *Life* magazine along with other breast cancer survivors.

At the time, Mikey and I were in Canton, Missouri, where I was doing a play. Now, ever since I had breast cancer, I had spoken about my experience, strictly as a volunteer thing, and it happened in the best possible way. I'd call somebody's cousin, or I'd go to a luncheon, or go to a benefit here and there. But there was no real pressure; I wasn't getting paid or anything, so I just spoke from my heart. Gradually—because I'm basically an improviser who sort of writes on her feet—a speech formed. But when the article appeared, I was approached by someone who told me, "You know, you could get paid for talking about your experience." I said, "No, I'm not good enough." Then later I thought, "I'd *better* get good enough."

I started calling people and making tapes and sending the *Life* magazine article around, and that year I began speaking for very small fees, taking the cheapest possible flight through three states when I was only going a hundred miles. And little by little, I learned how to do it and be at my best. I realized that I did have value and I could *give* that value; as I say in my speeches, if one woman at the end of my presentation says, "All right, I'll check out that lump," or "I'll get that mammogram," that's one *life*.

Traveling is difficult for me. I'd rather stay home and work on a TV series; that's still my goal and my dream. But after months and months on the road, I paid back all the money I borrowed, paid back all our debts, which was tens of thousands of dollars. Someone pointed out that this is unusual; a lot of people get money and still don't pay their debts. So I was very proud of myself, and it's given me great pleasure, especially to pay back people who are struggling now. A friend of mine in my hometown became a widow, and I sent her money and said, "Take this, and when you can help somebody else, you do it." That makes me feel good.

But it had been a long struggle since the day I woke up and realized that I had five dollars. Denny had been dead about a year and a half, I was $100,000 in debt, and I literally had five dollars. My friend Gary Dontzig called and said, "I'm coming over with five hundred dollars, and you don't have to pay me back." But as soon as I could, I sent him the money. He said, "You didn't have to pay me back," and I said, "I know, but something changed with that money. I was so grateful, and things started to get better after that. And now you can take that five hundred dollars and give it to someone else." Whatcha call yer "pay it forward."

20 don't look back

Coming Together

And then there was the night Lucy, Ethel and Ricky went to the Emmy Awards. (It was a scene right out of *I Love Lucy*). One Friday morning in July, my friend Rosanna called and said, "Congratulations! You won an Emmy." I, of course, said, "What a cruel thing to say to a widow," but I'll be damned if it wasn't true. I won an Emmy for outstanding voice-over performance for my role as the semi-lovely Edna Krabappel, Bart's teacher on *The Simpsons*, which really thrilled me, since I'm so proud to be a part of such a terrific show. It was somewhat bittersweet, since my sweetie wasn't here to share the celebration, and I decided to go with Julie Kavner (she plays Marge Simpson) and her husband David Davis (he created *The Bob Newhart Show*), two dear friends of long standing.

So I flew back from Missouri, where I was doing the female *Odd Couple* with Dawn Wells, rented me a nice sparkly dress, dug my beaded evening bag out of Mikey's Ninja Turtle sewer set (it was an interesting fashion choice for Donatello), and awaited the limo. Then I started to think (all this human interest stuff will make sense later), "Gee, it's a long ride to the beach to pick up the others; maybe I should pack some snacks." So I did, in a Bloomingdale's shopping bag. (You can take the girl out of Iowa, but you can't take Iowa out of the girl.)

193

So we drive to the beach, pick up Julie and David, and head for the ceremonies in Pasadena. The driver knew a shortcut (I believe it was through Utah) and we finally arrived, Late and Hungry (my attorneys), only to discover that there would be no food or drink until after the awards, lest someone overdo it. So we had tables of grown people fighting over stale chips and flat 7-Up. Some guy pulled a peach out of his pocket and was almost attacked. About two hours into the speeches, I started to laugh. I suddenly got this image of my darling Dennis sitting there in his tuxedo, starving; this could actually be the one night when he was just as glad to be dead. I laughed for ten minutes and then, of course, burst into tears.

Anyway, it did end, and we took off for my friends' fabulous restaurant in Pasadena, where I proceeded to eat lots of rich food and drink lots of red wine, not an easy task, since I never put down my Emmy. We get in the limo and David, dear David, who doesn't get out much, and when he does wants to make the most of it, kept saying, "Hey, it's early; let's go for pizza," which did not excite me or my stomach, and I said, "Excuse me, I'll be throwing up now." Which is what I did, in the aforementioned shopping bag.

Now, I am a woman who hates to litter, but on this point my limo-mates were adamant. As I opened the door of the limo at one in the morning in downtown L.A., I came face-to-face with a street person who had this brief look of glee on his face, as if to say "Wow, rich people are throwing Bloomingdale's bags out of limos. This is my lucky day." And that's the story of The Night I Won The Emmy, and you know what? I wasn't even embarrassed. I thought, "I'm fifty, menopausal, and a widow, three things I always wanted to be when I was a child growing up in Iowa."

Reconnections

Another loss was coming up. As long as Denny was alive, things were good between my mother and me. She couldn't believe our good fortune, because Dennis was every mother's dream for her daughter.

One of the great things about those years with Denny was that my mother loved me, and I loved her. Somehow the fact that I had a husband like Dennis validated me, and we got along great. She came out to visit often, because he was so terrific with her. And I thought, "Oh, look, isn't this wonderful? I've worked through all my mother stuff." And then when he died, I realized it was actually *him*; he was such a buffer for my family. And if my mother did say something hurtful, he was there to fix it with, "Don't you worry about it. We love you; don't you worry, it doesn't matter." Because I was so loved and felt so safe, I didn't worry, and nothing upset me.

But when he died, it all came back. The same old demons. I was supposed to go visit her, and we had this horrible fight and I said, "I'm not coming." And she said, "Well, what will I tell my friends? Your husband dies and you won't even come here. What will they think if you don't want to come and see your mother at a time like this?"

But I had learned one thing from losing Denny: that reconciliation with your family is everything. And as I started doing it with my mother-in-law, I thought, "At least I've got to try and do it with my mother." Because that had been the single rockiest relationship in my life. It shaped so much of who I am.

Maybe I've given my dad too much credit; that he shaped the good stuff about me, and my mother shaped the bad stuff. But I sure did buy into her idea that I was just not worthy of certain things in life. It's hard to believe she really didn't want them for me; I guess she thought it wasn't going to happen if I wasn't thinner and cuter. When I see pictures now of myself in high school, I was hardly the Troll from Tingley. I mean, I actually looked fine. But I used to think I was the fattest, ugliest girl on the planet. Because I wasn't thin and cute enough for my mother. Still, I didn't want to leave anything unresolved.

I was speaking in Des Moines not much later, and she came to see me. She heard my whole speech. And she loved it. And for the first time, she reached out to me. And the walls between us started to come down, and we started to connect to the good things in each other. And we started to heal.

Six months later she was dying, and I went back to see her.

For a while I was the only one there with her; my sister hadn't arrived yet. So I thought, "When I was a little girl, I used to wish she would rub my forehead when I didn't feel well; I'll do that for her." Well, she was in a coma, but she swatted my hand away. And then I remembered with Denny, how he was waiting for me to tell him, "It's okay, you can go; go to the light." So I said that to her. She came to, and only said one more thing: "Tell Marcia I'm not dying today."

It was so funny; it was deep and profound. And it made me laugh; it didn't make me feel bad. I'm here; my god, I'm here. Okay, you don't want to be rubbed, you don't want me to talk to you; I'll just be sitting in the corner. And then my sister came, and my brother, and Sherry did rub her head, and there we were with her, and then my mother stopped breathing. I remembered when that happened to Denny, so I said, "It's over." Then she started breathing again!

It was like a horror movie. You know, where the guys are half-dead, and then they come out of the sea? And the three of us went *"Waaahhhh!"* And then, of course, we laughed. That's the thing, too, about laughing—people think when there's a disaster or pain or tragedy, that laughing trivializes it, but it doesn't at all. It just makes it more human.

Her funeral was very profound for me because I wanted to speak, but I wanted to tell the truth. I couldn't lie; I wasn't going to stand up there and say that my mother and I loved each other so much and were so close. But I came to realize something wonderful. I received letters from people who said she was the best friend they ever had. These were young people, people her age: "Your mother used to listen to me and she'd make me feel so good about myself," and I thought, "What a shame she couldn't do that for her kids."

But it's a considerable achievement to be a good friend. So I was able to stand up in that church and say she loved her parents, and what a great friend she was. There was plenty to say, and it was very moving, and I felt a great deal of relief. Healing, redemption, reconciliation, whatever you want to call it—it's everything. In life, it's one of the few things we do have some control over.

Christmas 1996

Greetings.

I began the tradition of a biannual Christmas letter quite a long time ago. In the beginning, people were appalled. "A form letter?" they scoffed. Over the years, however, many of my friends came to enjoy these missives, which chronicled one woman's adventures, often providing more information about me than anyone wanted. And so it continues.

Last year was not my favorite. Two days after Thanksgiving my mother died of Crohn's disease in her hometown of Creston, Iowa, with her three children by her side. And you know what? It's hard to have both parents gone. It doesn't matter how old you are, or how difficult your relationship was; you're nobody's kid anymore. Nobody will ever again refer to my sister and me as "her girls."

Not long before she died (I wish it had been earlier), my mother and I healed our differences, and I truly came to appreciate her. She lived and died on her own terms and was a good and loyal friend. And she could turn a phrase. My personal favorites: "I don't like antiques; they're too old," and "I notice you talk to Mikey a lot; we didn't do that in my day."

Love,
Marcia

21 don't look back

→

Sing It, Frank!

My mother died just after Thanksgiving; I came home just before Christmas.

The first Christmas after Denny died, I refused to have a tree or celebrate. Everybody said, "You've got to have a tree for Mikey; you've got to." But because our Christmases had been so great, and putting up the tree had been so special for the two of us, I couldn't do it. Everybody was appalled, but I just couldn't do it. Instead I took Mikey to Club Med. Which was hilarious. I was still pretty much in shock; I was walking into walls. But Club Med was good—it was totally non-Christmassy.

The second year my sister said, "I'm going to go out and get a little tree for the kid," and she did.

Bringing Down the House

This year we put up the big tree with all the ornaments for the first time. Brett was staying with us, and the house was all done up for Christmas.

Mikey and I went out to see a movie. Brett stayed behind. She was in the back bedroom with Bingo the dog, having a martini or two and singing along with Frank Sinatra records. She began to hear an annoying noise, and she told me later that she kept asking Bingo, "Bingo, what the hell's that noise? Bingo?" (Hello... Brett... it's the smoke alarm.) Then she started singing along with Frank again. *"Sing it, Frank."* And she didn't know what the "annoying noise" was until she walked out of the bedroom and saw flames coming down the hall. She grabbed Bingo and ran out the back door.

Meanwhile, Mikey and I were coming home from the movies. "Oh, look Mikey, there's a fire on our street." "Oh, look, Mikey, there's a fire on our block." "Oh, Mikey, look, there's a fire in our house! *Aaaaarggggh!"*

There were three fire trucks up on the lawn, and Brett was outside sobbing. "I'm sorry, I'm sorry, oh, god, I'm sorry, I burnt down your house, oh, god, oh, god, you'll never forgive me, oh, god, I'm sorry!" And I was just stunned, stunned beyond belief. I walked in the house and the fireman said, "You can't know how lucky you are that no one died in this fire; there's so much smoke. I mean, we've pulled many bodies out of much less smoke than this."

The place looked like it had been bombed. They chopped through the roof; it collapsed later on. The kitchen and the living room, devastated. But Brett was in the back. She said the firemen tried to come in the front; they were chopping the front door down, which was incredibly strong, and she was screaming (swearing, of course) trying to get them to go around to the back, which was open. Finally they did, but they ruined the front door; they never did get it down. It was unbelievable.

My friend and neighbor Deb Engle had the key to John Malkovich's house, so we stayed there that night. I was certifiable; I just couldn't believe it.

I lost my wedding album, my wedding pictures, thirty years of books, thirty years of Christmas tree ornaments; I really hated that.

And we had to go live in the Oakwood Apartments in Koreatown. God, I hated that apartment! It was the bottom of the bottom. Thanks to "Mrs. O'Leary" Somers. "Bingo, what the hell's that noise? Sing it, Frank!"

What happened, apparently, was this: I had bought this huge rubber ball for Mikey, and we had one of those old-fashioned floor heaters with individual thermostats. I'd always been told they were dangerous, but I loved them—you could warm up the room and then turn it off—plus, we couldn't afford central heating. But the grille could get very hot.

Brett used to come in the house and say, "It's cold in here!" And she'd turn the thermostat up to, like, ninety-five, so those flames were constantly licking. The rubber ball must have rolled onto the grate and melted. She never noticed it was sitting on the grate when she turned the heat up. Mikey loved that stupid ball.

One thing that was sweet: my neighbors all said, "We wanted to be out on the street for you when you got home, because we knew it wasn't going to be a good moment for you." And they were all lined up, my neighbors all lined up. I was very touched.

The next day, the ghouls arrived—the people who want your business. The repairers, the fire restorers—they came right into the house. My neighbor Roger tried to get rid of them, but they're so thick-skinned. They want to sign you up while you're in shock. Ghouls! Talk about ambulance chasers.

Fortunately (if there was anything fortunate in this experience) I had this excellent fire insurance policy dating back from the days when I was rich. The first thing the company did for us was arrange temporary accommodations in the Koreatown Oakwood Apartments.

Garbage Girl

The only good thing about the Koreatown Oakwood Apartments was that they had a garbage chute, which meant you could have unlimited garbage. Because garbage became my life. It's all I looked forward to; that I could come home and get rid of everything. Plus, if it was raining, you didn't have go out in it to get rid of your garbage. I made several trips to the garbage chute every day. I love garbage day anyway.

Mikey calls me "garbage girl." But, as bad as the fire was, something happened there one night where I truly almost lost my mind.

Mikey was in the second grade by now, and he had just moved to the magnet school. He had gone from the extremely loose approach of Play Mountain Place to this new school. It wasn't all that rigid, but he came home one day and said, "I hope you're happy; they made me sit in that chair so long today I almost went mad." (He has never used that word before or since. This is in the second grade!) He had a great teacher, Monette Morgan—they called the teachers by their first names there, too—but he was not adjusting at all. He felt like, "What's the matter with these people? Sit still here for an hour? What, are they crazy?!"

And he was meeting all new friends, several of whom were going through difficult times. I was constantly being approached by these new (to me) mothers: "Hi, you don't know me. I'm Bernice, and I wondered if my child could spend the night with you for three nights. Here, this is him. Say hello—say hello to Mrs. Hawley." And I would mutter: "Well, I'm not in the best shape here, and I don't have any room, and—" But they were relentless.

So this one time, a woman came up to me. She was the magnet school coordinator. Her name was Kyla Hinson and her son's name was Kyle, and they were African-American, and the little boy was extremely dark. I've gone on to have a friendship with both of them, but I didn't know her at all back then. Anyway, she comes up and says, "Hello, you don't know me, but I wonder if my child could come and spend the night with you tonight?"

So there he is, he and Mikey, lying on this rollout bed, sleeping on white sheets. I happen to come out in the middle of the night, and I cannot find the kid. And I think, "My house has burned, my husband is dead, and now I've lost somebody's child and I don't even know their last name." And I start running up and down the hall, pounding, pounding on doors: "Have you seen a little black boy? He's a little black boy? *He'salittleblackboy!*"

Oh, my god! I don't know my neighbors, they don't know me,

it's three o'clock in the morning, but he's gone! I truly thought I would lose my mind. I come back in, and the kid is back. He had moved to the dark sofa and shut his eyes, and I couldn't see him. Now he's opened his eyes and moved back onto the white sheets.

When I finally got up enough nerve to tell the mother, she howled. "Oh, wait till I tell my husband!"

The Joys of Sisterhood

By now my sister and I weren't getting along at all. My mother had just died, and we were both trying to cope with our feelings. It was just awful. Sherry said I was certifiable. I said, "I can't go to The Bin; I've already been there." She thought everybody had to be protected from me because I was so nuts. And I don't doubt that I was a little crazy; I was certainly angry. We would get into these awful fights. Finally one night I screamed, "Get out!"

And she screamed back, "No!"

"*Get out!*"

"*No!*"

"*GET OUT!*"

"*NO!*"

My sister and I, oh, god, we fought and fought and fought. But we stayed together. You have to give it to us; we couldn't be less alike, and yet we have been totally committed to this sisterhood. People get estranged and they stop speaking, but life's too short, and this bond is too deep, so we keep going.

You meet your husband and children well into your life, and usually lose your parents halfway through, but your siblings are there from the beginning to the end. My sister Sherry is so precious to me.

When You Hit Bottom, Whether You Bounce Back Up or Break in Half is Up to You

But what a misery it was living in Koreatown! It was unbelievably hot, there were all these clashing smells from various international cuisines. It seemed like the worst place in the world. It was endless. And having to move there after the fire was just one loss too many for me.

And, boy, did things start to hit the emotional fan. Oh, sure, there were all the old standby menopausal dwarves: Crabby, Weepy, Fatty, Crazy; but now there appeared a new dwarf: Angry. Boy, was I pissed: at the universe, at myself, and, for the first time, at Dennis for dying and leaving me alone to deal with this… this… *life*. Rational? Of course not. Reasonable? No, but then I have never felt the need to be reasonable.

It all culminated one Tuesday in February in a fast food drive-through line. "My Epiphany at McDonalds," by Marcia Wallace. (You can take the girl out of Iowa, etc., etc.) Anyway, I was late, the service was slow, and all my dwarves were in the car with me. Plus the guy in back was honking up a storm. I asked the girl, "Now, you gave me ketchup, right? Lots of ketchup; I want ketchup." She said, "Yes, yes, ketchup," and waved me on. I left the line, back on the road, opened the bag, and, voila, no ketchup.

I, of course, did what any sensible menopausal widow would have done: I sobbed and screamed for thirty minutes, at myself, my life and my darling husband. "Damn you, Dennis Hawley, damn you! You died and left me with *no ketchup!*" And then, when I had no voice left, I started to laugh. I laughed until my shoes were wet. I cried and I laughed and somehow my heart started to open just a little, and the healing began. What felt like a nervous breakdown turned out to be a nervous breakthrough.

My dear neighbors Roger and Gene had warned me in the first days after the fire, "Don't sign anything." But one day a woman named Peggy showed up, telling me she was the owner of a fire restoration business. I realize that I didn't ask her the questions I should have because she was a woman and I was so impressed she had her own business; I didn't ask her for references. I learned a very important lesson: just because you're a woman doesn't mean that you can't be as much of a shyster as the next guy. She was duplicitous, she was dishonest and she was inept. Not one of my favorite people. Who knew there was such a thing as a fire restoration company? They came in, crated everything up, took everything away, and then decided what was worth keeping. But she lost half my stuff!

Luckily, I had a great fire policy. The first thing I said to the adjuster was, "I'm so pissed off; I've had this fur coat that I can't wear because I'm afraid Loretta Swit's going to throw paint on me, and it's been in the house for years, and I just loaned it to somebody to wear in a play. It was worth thousands of dollars. If it had been in the house I could have been paid for it." Somebody said, "Well, you could *pretend* it was." But I figure after you've had a fire, you don't want to be making *no* bad causes.

I'm amazed at the number of people who try to cheat after bad luck happens. I don't get it. But maybe if it doesn't bother you, it doesn't bother you. It would bother me. I believe in cause and effect. Telling the insurance adjuster about the fur coat turned out to be the smartest thing I've ever done. Because I was honest, they were great with me and gave me the total replacement value of everything—and it was several hundred thousand dollars.

Careerwise, I'm still doing *The Simpsons* and other voice-overs, and yearn to do another sitcom. It's still the best job in the world for an actor. I've also been on the circuit speaking as a breast cancer survivor, mostly during October, which is Breast Cancer Awareness Month. I was in thirty-seven cities in six weeks. I'd love to spread these appearances out into other months, but I'd have to get another disease. I don't think so.

Meryl Streep continues to be envious of my "art film career," most especially my appearance in the movie *Ed*. I was cut out; I'm sure it's because I was so dazzling that I pulled focus from the monkey. In truth, if my movies are released at noon, by four o'clock they're in the video stores.

Another one of the things I'm very proud of is my healing and reconciliation with my mother-in-law. Looking back on Dennis's illness, I've realized that all those times I thought she was just being mean to me, she was, of course, watching her darling child die.

After her husband died, I reached out to her. And she said to me, "I don't know why I was mean to you; I don't know why I felt that way." So gradually we've come back together. I wanted to do it for my son, because she's his only living grandparent, and I wanted to do it for my Denny, because we were the two women he loved most. He would be very proud of us both. I was able to help her when her husband died, and I've been able to help her now, since her son Tom died of cancer.

She's eighty-five years old, and she's amazing. She keeps going, and she's incredibly courageous. She's determined to have happy moments and embrace the life that she has left. But it must be terribly hard. We have gotten to be so close; it goes to show you what's possible in life, and that the key to everything is healing and forgiveness.

One of the things Denny's death taught me is don't leave things unsaid, undone, unfinished, unresolved.

Of course I've had good times since Denny died. I've had great laughs; I've had trips; I've had wonderful times with my friends, my family, my son; but there are times when I feel that the best part of me died with him. And I'm constantly struggling to recapture that part. But everybody does it in their own way, in their own time.

22 don't look back

Starting Over

In 1998, I finished my prune tour. Yes, I was the spokesperson for the California Prune Growers. And if you think it's easy to work prunes into the conversation at 6:30 a.m. on *Good Morning Butte*, you're crazy.

There is, however, a whole prune underground out there. And even though I enjoyed it and was able to tie it into my breast cancer message—it's a low-fat, high-fiber food, and they give money to breast cancer research—still, I had to work those prunes in, work them in, 'cause I was the Prune Gal. I wanted to be the Queen of Broadway, a diva; thirty years later, I had become the Prune Gal.

But it was all part of earning a living. This is a little fringe-y, in the show business realm. But they wouldn't have asked me to be the Prune Gal if I hadn't had a certain amount of success in my chosen field. So therefore I do like to think that it's all tied together, that somehow there's a life-to-life connection, and that maybe you connect to one person in one town by something you say, even if it's about prunes. And basically it was fun.

But I'll tell you something I'm able to lead a rich full life without, and that's one more appearance as the Prune Gal in a grocery store. I used to have to sit there with my prune samples and my eight-by-ten glossies under a big banner that said "COME MEET MARCIA

WALLACE AND GET YOUR PRUNE SAMPLES HERE," and I'd have people come up to me, and I'd get ready to sign my photo, and they'd say, "Excuse me, could you tell me where the frozen spinach is?" So it's just fine with me that I don't have to attend any more of those supermarket openings. (Sorry, it really is over, so don't bother asking.)

But there's one thing that helped me get through everything I had to deal with during this extremely difficult period: *I love my boy.* It was such a hard time for both of us, but he got it together long before I did. After the fire, he wouldn't leave my side. He paged me, called me, followed me around, stuck to me like glue, and then got up one morning, said, "Well, I'm through my phase!" and went away for the weekend. What a kid! Lord knows there have been so many times when I've felt pretty long in the tooth to be the parent of a boy Mikey's age, but to be honest, anything I couldn't do in my fifties, I couldn't do in my twenties, either.

Why Pyromaniacs Make the Best Maids

So we finally moved back into our house after the fire. It was beautiful, it was clean, it was new. And I was thinking not long after we moved back in how much Denny had loved his house and how pleased he would have been with how it looked after the restoration. Then, since he had known better than anyone just how homemaking-impaired I am, I imagined him saying to me, "Oh, honey, I'm sorry, but we just had to burn it and start from scratch."

So we came back to our lovely home, which looked exactly the same, only clean. Some people told me then that maybe I should have left this house. Although the experts advise you not to make any major moves for at least a year after a death or trauma. I wondered if staying in this house would keep me back. I didn't think so. I fought like hell to keep this house for any number of reasons, especially for Mikey. If I had given it up, I'd never have been able to buy another one—I'd still be out there paying rent, with no deductions, with no hope of ever coming up with a down payment. I've owned a house since I was twenty-eight years old, which is a considerable achievement, and it's continued to be a real big part of my feeling of security.

It was a joy to be home again after that apartment. I had thought I could never forget that place and the trauma of the fire, but all that dissolved fairly quickly. Sherry moved out into her own little guesthouse, so it was just Mikey and me. We'd been out of the house for eight months. Poor Bingo was so lonely in the kennel we'd had to keep him in, he almost died. Once we moved back into the house, we all felt like romping.

The Courtship of Mikey's Mother

For a long time after I lost Denny, I felt dead from the neck down, and my libido went the way of my memory and my attention span. Plus I had gained forty pounds, which is not conducive to getting sex in any city. I mean, even in my earlier days when I didn't have a fella, or wasn't even thinking about sex, I was aware of my senses. But I realized that in the time since Denny had died, I hadn't been aware of things like the sun on my face or the way music sounded; I hadn't been touched or thought about being touched. Yep, dead from the neck down, and eating was my *job*. I did get a lot of good hugs from Mikey, however.

So I just thought, "I guess that's it for me." I had had a lot of good encounters in my youth, and a great relationship with my hubby, and that was probably going to be it. Well, then, lo and behold, out of the blue, I started to feel something. And I thought, "What in the world is going on here?" At first I thought I was having a stroke, and then I realized it was an actual sexual urge. It got worse and it increased and increased and intensified and intensified till I got very close to running down the street with my dress over my head. Which I think probably is a sight no man should see and live. I mean, I thought nobody but Denny was ever going to see my thighs again. I wasn't too fond of the way I look naked, and I'd been out of the sexual loop for decades. "Ewwwww," I thought, social diseases and life-threatening diseases and worse, the dreaded condoms, which I loathe, loathe, loathe. Let me repeat that.

Anyway, I was sure about one thing. I was not about to take off my clothes in front of no guy in this town, so I said, "Okay... well, maybe a woman." Now, granted, I'd never been with a woman, but I was pretty sure I wouldn't be so self-conscious about the way I looked, and a touch is a touch, and what the hell. But amazingly enough, after thirty years in show business, I knew gay guys galore but only one lesbian, and I hadn't seen her in a while, and I felt funny about calling her up and saying, "How are you? Uh, listen... I'm looking to make my re-entry into the sensual realm, and I thought maybe with a woman. Any ideas?"

More and more I continued to think about it, and I thought, "I've got to get touched. I've got to get touched! I cannot be running into the night, screaming, 'Touch me, touch me, hold me, hold me!'"

I was in Dallas giving a speech and I made plans to have dinner with my old friend Larry Randolph. People I had talked to about this lesbian idea either thought I was kidding or were shocked, and these were guys who had been with *goats*. What were they shocked about, for heaven's sake? I was just talking about a little human contact. But Larry was more open-minded. So I told him, and he says, "Hmmm." I said, "Larry, you know lesbians?" He said, "Well, yes, I do. But you didn't give me enough notice here. But I have a lesbian neighbor; she often sits out on her stoop. Let's go see if she's there."

It was like "Ricky and Lucy Look for Lesbians." His neighbor wasn't on her stoop, so I said, "What about a bar?" I never even went to straight bars; I don't know from bars. But he said, "I don't know; I think I know where there's a lesbian bar." So we went to look for it, and it was now a place to get your nails done.

Finally we found one. Well, please, it was just hilarious. We went inside, and there were three little lesbianettes. They were *so* young. They looked at me and said, "Oh, my god, it's Mrs. Krabappel!" Well, we collapsed in a great heap of laughter, and went back to see if his lesbian was on the stoop, and she wasn't. So I figured, this is clearly not supposed to happen.

Then I went home and thought, "I'm a woman with a mission. I've got to get touched." So I called my friend Bryan Peterson, who is also a big talker about his lesbian friends. Well, he couldn't think of any, either. And I said, "You're not leaving this house until you get me a lesbian." So I brought out the champagne and said, "Now, get on that phone."

He says, "What am I supposed to tell them?"

I said, "You tell them you have a friend who's a widow, who's looking to make a re-entry into the sexual realm, and feels that she could trust and feel more comfortable with a woman. This is not a change in lifestyle, this is an adventure for someone who might be interested." Well, please, now it's Ricky and Lucy and Ethel.

Eventually it became clear that nobody was interested, nobody knew any, or they couldn't get them on the phone, or they weren't on the stoops, and I thought, "Well, I guess this is just not for me."

So since I couldn't make this happen for myself, and since I still wasn't ready to take off my clothes in front of a man, I decided to do the next most sensible thing: I decided to start collecting Beanie Babies. I'm sure so many women have had to face that difficult choice: "Hmmm, let me see, what'll it be? Lesbian sex or Beanie Babies?"

So, I of course—never being a woman of moderation—went right out and bought hundreds of Beanie Babies, even bought furniture for them. It was pathetic; my friend Robyn said, "Hon, we're going to have to do an intervention." There you have it: "The Return of the Libido." Aren't you glad you asked?

At Least I'm Trying

Somebody once asked me if I thought I was a good person. I answered that I did, and I do, actually. I basically wish people well. I feel that I'm supportive of friends. I've been a good daughter, a good sister. I was a good wife; I was a good partner to my hubby. But I realize that at the very bottom of the list, in terms of how I view myself, is the way I view myself as a mother. Most of the time I haven't seen myself as a very good one. I didn't set out to do this alone. I don't like doing it alone; it makes me feel very lonely.

We were a great match, Denny and I. We brought two different things to the party: I was spontaneous; he was structured. But to be honest about parenthood—first of all, I think it's highly overrated a lot of the time. I've tried sometimes to connect with other mothers and say, "Don't you ever feel trapped? Don't you ever want to just run out of the house and get in your car and drive forever? Don't you just want to *beat him bloody* sometimes?" And everybody says, "Ohhh, don't be silly." I have yet to find somebody who'll say, *"Sure."* So I end up feeling like I'm either the world's worst parent, or everybody else is not being entirely truthful.

Of course the older Mikey gets, the more attitude he gets, which I *really* love. And this is a good kid; I've got a *good* kid. After Denny died there wasn't much I could enforce, but gradually, over the years I've added other boundaries, which Mikey's not happy about. Kids need them. I try only to add what I can be consistent about.

Another thing I *love* about being a parent: everybody you're close to (and some you're not) never hesitate to tell you how they think you're doing. Read my lips: who asked you? So sometimes I feel very thin-skinned. But then I think, "You've got to just ease up on yourself." And I realize that, in truth, he had those first three or four years with his dad and me; I was so happy then, so much more fun. But these things happen.

So there you go, it's me and Mikey. I think, bottom line, for all the mistakes I've made—and I've made thousands—the interesting thing to me is to realize that I've tried very hard to stop the cycle that began in my own family. I've resolved things with my mother and father and moved on.

In New York City a few years ago, Mikey and I went to visit the *USS Intrepid,* the aircraft carrier my dad served on in World War II.

Which he talked about till the day he died. He was a signalman; he used to bring the planes in. Half the time they crashed, people would die—we can't even conceive of it—we were war babies, but we don't have any idea what it was like. I was so sorry I'd shined him on. *"I won the war, Marcia."* Yes, yes, Dad, we know you won the war.

And I suddenly had a million questions: Who did you know? Where did you sleep? Were you scared? Did you see anyone die in front of you? And I was so sorry that I had never let him talk about it, never thought of any questions to ask him. Now I was just desperate to know, going up the same steps he walked up while the bombs were falling (the *Intrepid* was bombed five or six times, and never sank). He had concussions; he had all kinds of head injuries. It was very, very profound and moving to be on that ship with my son, his grandson.

The one thing I can say without question is that Mikey has a mom who doesn't give up. I just *don't give up.* I've kept him safe and clothed, in a good school. He's seen the wolf at the door, and somehow I managed to save us. Hopefully he'll remember all that and it will be as important to him as the time I smacked him on the arm and screamed *"I hate my life!"*

But the great thing about Mikey is that he absolutely won't take it. He says, "I don't deserve this. How can you speak that way to your only child?" That's very, very good. And he's right. These are scary times to be a kid.

As he's gotten older, Mikey hasn't developed much of a resemblance to Michael J. Fox, so I guess he doesn't look much like his biological father. In any case, he's growing up to be a real heartbreaker. By the time he was twelve, the girls had already started to love him. Just love him. That same year, I went to one of those awful school meetings because I was in charge of the silent auction. (Just give me your piano; I'll get rid of it.) And everyone was saying, "Oh, that Mikey. He's so great; we've got to auction off a date with him." And he *was* great, and continues to be. He's funny and he's smart and talented. And kind. I'm *real* proud of him. And I know Denny is, too.

23 don't look back

Christmas 1998

Greetings,

Over the years, since I first began my first every-other-year Christmas letter tradition in 1980, I have written to you about life and love, sickness and health, careers, travel, mind, body, spirit, relationships, and those ever popular three m's: middle-aged marriage, motherhood and menopause. One thing's for sure, they were usually newsy as the dickens. So I'm not sure what this says about me these days, but here's what I've got so far this year:

Hello. I'm older. I'm fatter. I'm crabbier. Merry Christmas.

Not very festive, is it? Surely I can do better than that:

'98 started with an attack of "vertigo." That would be the malady, not the movie. I got up one day and fell over; ever so attractive. At first I thought it was just another of my menopausal dwarves. You know, Dizzy—to go along with Crabby, Sweaty, Dippy, Sleepy, Hostile and Perverse. (Trust me on this; I'm convinced we're all hormones away from being serial killers.)

But it turned out to be a lovely virus. Eventually, the flu symptoms abated and the dizziness went on and on and on, longer than El Nino. I discovered there is quite a dizzy underground out there; who knew? I had people tell me they had been dizzy for six, count 'em, six years. Such good news. At one point, I thought, "Well, if I'm going to have this forever, I should at least wake up some morning looking like Kim Novak in that movie," but I think it was James Stewart who had the actual vertigo. Then I thought, "Oh, the way things are going, I'll wake up looking like him and acting like her."

The only time during all those months that I was totally dizzy-free was when I was flying somewhere to give a speech, but since I'm a little long in the tooth to become a flight attendant (I am crabby enough, however), I had to work it out on the ground. And sure enough, I woke up on June 20th and it was gone. I was, however, twenty pounds heavier from all those times I fell off my treadmill into the refrigerator; what's a girl to do? And—how do I put this—I am not a woman who needed to gain twenty pounds.

So what happens next? People magazine called and asked me to be on their October 23rd 1998 cover, along with several beautiful, talented and inspirational breast cancer survivors. I was, of course, honored. I made several phone calls to see if I could lose forty pounds in a weekend, but even in Hollywood that's not possible. So there I was, looking very well groomed, well coiffed, well made-up, and only slightly smaller than the state of Wisconsin.

The journey continues. I try to give myself some slack. I like to think I am a deep and thoughtful person, always thinking of important things, like human relationships, world events, the fate of us all… But I'm going to be truly honest; I haven't thought about anything in my life as much as I've thought of food: what I'm eating, when I'm eating it, and "Are you going to finish those French fries?"

And the older I get, the more I've started to turn into my parents, talking wistfully of past meals: "Oh, gosh, I remember that twice-baked potato I had back in '89; it was as big as my head." And giving way too much information to waitresses: "Now, there's no shellfish in that oatmeal, is there? I have an allergy, you know. I'll blow up like a poison dart." (As my mother used to say.)

I am, however, beginning to reverse my tubby trend. Sometimes I think I've stayed fat because I'm flunking widowhood and can't get over *the loss of my beloved Dennis, and if I lose weight I'd feel too vulnerable. But I would like to get married again. I loved being married. However, I don't want to date, and I don't want anyone to see my thighs, so that shortens the list considerably.*

I took Mikey (who is agewise into double digits) to New York City this summer and we had a great time. It was such a thrill for me to show him a city I know so well and love so much, but I thought it might be overwhelming for a kid. Shows what I know; there we were, standing in Times Square surrounded by all those lights, and he said, "Oh, Mom, I love Manhattan. It's my kind of town."

I was on the road a lot this year, still speaking as a breast cancer survivor, and I also added a sponsorship. Hold onto your fiber... I am now the spokesperson for the California Prune Growers. Oh, sure, it's not quite what I had in mind when I took off for the Big Apple to conquer Broadway, but as my dad used to say, "Don't look back, we're not going that way."

He also said, "If I don't see you again, the mule is yours," so not everything he said was profound, but he did give me some awfully good advice, my personal favorite being, "Hon, don't have no cheap dreams."

Have a spectacular holiday and new year, and a great new millennium... YIKES.

Love,
Marcia and Mikey

24 don't look back

Christmas 2000

Greetings,

Well, here's the deal: I had higher hopes for the new millennium, so I think I'll start over again in 2001. As for the past year, Mikey is getting hormones, I'm losing them... what's wrong with this picture? Of course, it's always been my heart's desire to be in my middle years living with a teenage boy with attitude. Last week, he told me he wanted to be an actor. I said, "Fine, act like you like me."

Recently I said to Mikey, "You know, honey, we don't appreciate each other enough, so let's start doing that. I'll go first: you have a good heart. Okay, your turn." He thought for a minute and said, "Well, you take me places." I said, "Okay, my turn: you've never lied to me." And then he said, "Listen, are we going to wrap this up soon? I'm running out of ideas." The kid makes me laugh.

How's my social life, you ask? Well, I almost went out with this guy who was recently separated, but he decided he would rather cheat than date and went back to his wife. Then my confidence took another hit around Halloween. (My least favorite holiday; I'm not crafty and my only successful costume was in drag. I looked like a cross between Wayne Newton and the Pillsbury Dough Boy.) Anyway, after two hours spent in a Halloween store with about six hundred kids, we leave and I discover I've been towed. Now, I seem to be genetically incapable of

reading street signs, and they only get more confusing, especially in L.A.:
"No parking after 4 p.m. unless you're Lithuanian and it's Tuesday."
Puhleeeze.

Anyway, the kids ran ahead (one of the kid perks—they run, so
you don't have to), we caught up with the tow truck, and the guy let me
pay the fine there. Then this other towee comes over to Mikey and says,
"Listen, little boy, next time you read the sign; your grandmother is
old." I said, "Hello? Towed and insulted? And you're no spring chicken
yourself." He said, "Oh, I am French. In France, everybody over fifty is
old." Gee, thanks. Let me run right over to Gay Paree.

And talk about unnerving, I went back to Creston, Iowa, for my
fu... fu... fortieth high school reunion last summer and had a fabulous
time. I remember my mother going to her fortieth, and I said to her,
"Well, I can't believe any of you are still alive." Oh, kids, be very careful
what you say, it will come back and bite you in your large Midwestern
ass.

We had a wonderful time. Mikey loves it there, and every time I
go back I appreciate it more and more. And here's the shocker: Mikey
spent days doing manual labor on a friend's farm. He baled hay, for
heaven's sake. I was so hoping his attack of Midwestern work ethic
would survive the plane ride home, but noooo!

Workwise, I'm still on The Simpsons, and travel around the
country speaking. (They actually hire me; I don't just show up in a city
and start talking.) Even though I haven't been on camera for a year or
so, I still get recognized. Why, just last month, this guy comes up to me
at an airport and says, "It's you, right?" I say, "Well, actually it is. Uh-
huh." He says, "Wait a minute; I gotta go get my wife." So he runs off,
he drags this poor woman back, he says, "See, I told you it's her." She
says, "It is not! It is not that nurse from Poughkeepsie."

I was, however, recognized by a blind guy last summer in
Washington, D.C. I was asking directions and heard this voice behind
me say, "Aren't you Marcia Wallace?" I turn around and there stands
this blind gentlemen with a cane. I reply, "Why, yes I am." He said, "I
thought so," and off he tapped. It made my day, but I thought later I

shouldn't have let him get away. I always say I don't want to date and I don't want anybody to see my thighs. Well, HELLO, this guy would have been perfect.

I'm very pleased to say I've finished my book. It's called (to quote my father) Don't Look Back, We're Not Going That Way. *I so look forward to selling the book so I can start "selling the book." After all, I was spokesperson for the California Prune Growers, and if I can work prunes into the conversation at six in the morning on* Good Morning, Akron, *I do feel I can promote my own story, which certainly includes the journey of Mikey's adoption.*

He's grown very close to his birth sister, Ashley. They visit, they phone, they e-mail; they'll have each other always. We had what would qualify as an unusual group gathering for Thanksgiving last year: myself, my son, his birth mother from Louisiana, his birth sister, and my nephew, who's on parole. I realize an extended family like this is not for everybody, but here's my feeling: I'm his mother. There's all kinds of families these days, and you can't have too many people who love you.

Here's to a joyous holiday and a spectacular 2001.

Love,

Marcia and Mikey

Epilogue

(or whatever the hell they call it)

We all know what's happened on a larger scale since I finished this book. The world as we knew it will never be the same again.

As for my own personal journey, on November 1, 2002, I turned sixty and had to lie down for months. No one was more surprised than I, having always been a gal who embraced each and every year, but this one brought me to my knees (and being sixty, it was *reeal* hard to get up again).

I heard someone say sixty was the new fifty. I'd be thrilled if it turned out to be the new fifty-nine and a half.

And sixty seems to bring with it *sooo* many perks. I've survived a lot (see title of book) but here're words I never thought I'd type: It seems I have a senile bladder.

"What's that?" I asked the doctor. "It can't remember when it's peed and doesn't recognize the other organs?"

He just stared at me.

That always-fascinating and ever-cranky Bette Davis was right when she said getting older is not for sissies, and my, but there's got to be a better name for that diagnosis.

The Old Mother and the Teenager

Mikey is now fifteen, and the following story pretty much sums up what's doing with him these days. He got off the bus recently and told me he was sure he had SARS, and I should get him to the emergency room immediately. It was serious, he assured me, so we better get moving — who knew how much time he had? I reassured him that it was just a cold, and of course if he got a fever we'd go to the doctor, but he said that wasn't good enough. He could go (snap) just like *that*, and then he said:

"If I die before I have sex, you'll have to live with that the rest of your life."

Does Anybody See a Career Trend Here?

What's coming next? In truth, I have no idea. It would be great if I got a new series, or met Mr. Right Number Two, which may or may not happen. But maybe it's okay to be a work in progress; certainly I'm somebody who's constantly trying to learn. Ten years ago, I was a devastated widow with a little kid, a house that was ready to be fore-closed, and a hundred thousand dollars' worth of debts. Now all that's paid off and my house is secure. And I'm opening up to new possi-bilities. Who knows what's around the corner? I feel ready to find out. You know me, hon, I'm a scrappy gal. And I'm not looking back... 'cause I'm not going that way.

Careerwise of late, I continue to speak as a breast cancer sur-vivor. I played the sassy White House maid in Comedy Central's *That's My Bush*. And I have been traveling the country doing many the production of *The Vagina Monologues*.

And of course, Edna Krabappel still lives.

That's My Bush, created by those equal-opportunity *South Park* offenders Trey Parker and Matt Stone, was a great gig and a hilarious show, although the franchise pretty much ended with 9/11. I loved every minute of it, though, and even the audition was wacky. I was the very last person seen after they auditioned the young, the black, the white, the fat, the thin, for over four months. Anyway, I arrived, signed in, and ran to the bathroom, where I promptly got locked in the bathroom stall. (It's a shame *Bette* got cancelled; this cried out to be an episode.)

There's me pounding and yelling to no avail, so I lie down and try to slide under the door, but still being on the pudgy side, I promptly get stuck and am lying there thinking, "Jeez, what a career I'm having." It seemed like I was there long enough for two kids to finish college, but finally I shimmed under and ran frazzled into the audition with quite the story and an energy level off the Richter scale.

And I got the job that very day.

They didn't snap me up that fast for *The Vagina Monologues*. I knocked on their door for a very long time. I believe I was on the list after the brunette from *Petticoat Junction* and Telly Savalas's niece. But call they finally did, and I have talked about my vagina in cities all over the country. It has been a glorious, life-changing experience. Thank you, Eve Ensler.

Now, it's been a continuing source of disappointment to me, but I don't usually attract yer stage-door johnnies; that is, until *Vagina Monologues*. Oh, sure, there's the occasional mother-son duo that shows up with six teeth between them, clutching a twenty-year-old photo of me and Herve Villechaize that I sign, as Herve isn't available.

But it's rare.

Until two *extremely* mature gentlemen waited for me as I left the theater. We're talking *old* here, with lots of polyester, open shirts and gold chains, only add sunken chests to the mix. *Very* attractive. They were "Old and Older." And guess what? *Father* and *son.*

Hank:	Miss Walters, I'm Hank, and this is my son Ed, and we're big fans of yours.
Me:	Well, actually, it's Wallace, but thanks so much.
Hank:	Guess how old I am? Go ahead, guess.
Me:	Oh, gosh, I don't know, Hank. Sixty-two.
Hank:	Hah! I'm a hundred. One hundred years old. And Ed

here is gonna be seventy-nine in August.

Me: Well, imagine that. So nice to meet y—

Hank: You don't believe me, do you? Here.

He then proceeded to whip out his driver's license. Well, "whip" is not exactly the word; it took him about six minutes. Very, very long minutes. And sure enough, he was born April 14, 1902. You'll all be relieved to hear that the license expired in 1982. His boy drives him now; he just uses the license to convince people he really is 100, because, as Hank puts it, "Most people think I look like Harrison Ford."

Uh-huh.

Hank told me, "Me and Ed just loved the show and all that vagina talk. It's like I've always told him, 'Life begins from the navel down.'"

He then suggested the three of us get together for some "fun." Well, by this time, I am gouging my fingers into my leg to keep from laughing or screaming or both, and I finally make my escape. But now, the image of the three of us together is seared forever in my brain, and I am again looking for that twenty-four-hour drive-through lobotomat.

Well, it's a beginning.

I do know that doing this wonderful play, which is so celebratory about being real, interesting, sexual, and grown-up women, has tapped into something deep in my life that I thought was gone forever.

I don't have a clue what to do with all these new feelings, short of running down the street with my dress over my head. I am, after all, a seriously middle-aged, not-even-remotely-thin woman who's chin-challenged, living in a town and a time that worships the young, the thin and the beautiful. What are the chances?

But, hey, in a world of millions, I found my one true love, and he loved me right back, deeply and madly.

It could happen again.

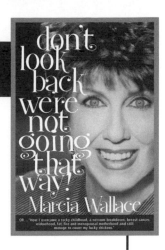